Hitler's Werewolves

Hitler's Werewolves

The Story of the Nazi Resistance Movement
1944–1945

by
CHARLES WHITING

STEIN AND DAY/*Publishers*/New York

First published in 1972
Copyright © 1972 Charles Whiting as *Werewolf*
Library of Congress Catalog Card No. 72-187301
All rights reserved
Printed in the United States of America
Stein and Day/*Publishers*/7 East 48 Street, New York, N.Y. 10017
ISBN 0-8128-1468-1

CONTENTS

MAPS

Drawn by Patrick Leeson

ILLUSTRATIONS

ACKNOWLEDGEMENTS

Understandably some of the people who gave me the information on which this book is based do not want their names to be mentioned. However, I should like to take this opportunity of thanking those people who supplied me with details and can afford to have their names published. In particular, I am grateful to Frau Oppenhoff, wife of the murdered Chief Burgomaster of Aachen; Dr. Gierlich, Chief Public Prosecutor in the same city for allowing me to see his files; ex-Colonel Otto Skorzeny, the rescuer of Mussolini; Major-General Sir Kenneth Strong, Eisenhower's Chief-of-Intelligence; Dr Simons, editor-in-chief of the *Aachener Volkszeitung*, and Dr Deschner, editor-in-chief of *Berthelsmann Sachbuchverlag*; Mr J. Saive, the brother of the Werewolves' first victim; and, in particular, Herr Erich Morgenschweiss, who was once a member of Adolf Hitler's Werewolves.

C.W.

BIBLIOGRAPHY

Otto Skorzeny: *Wir Kampften—Wir Verloren* (Ring Verlag, Siegburg).

John Toland: *The Last 100 Days* (Random House, New York).

Kenneth Strong: *Intelligence at the Top* (Cassell, London).

Dwight D. Eisenhower: *Crusade in Europe* (Doubleday, New York).

Rodney Minott: *The Fortress that Never Was* (Holt, Rinehart & Winston, New York).

Albert Speer: *Memoirs* (Macmillan, New York).

Omar Bradley: *Soldier's Story* (Holt, Rinehart & Winston, New York).

George Patton: *War As I Knew It* (Houghton Mifflin, Boston).

Charles Codman: *Drive* (Little, Brown, Boston).

H. R. Trevor-Roper: *The Last Days of Hitler* (Macmillan, New York).

Bernard Pol: *Oppenhoff* (Cologne).

Saul Padover: *A Psychologist in Germany*.

And various articles in the following newspapers and magazines: *Aachener Nachrichten, Aachener Volkszeitung, Neue Revue, Grenzecho, Die Glocke, Vierteljahrschrift f. Zeitgeschichte.*

Inset map:
Vijlen
Vaals
Wolfhaag
Gemmenich
AACHEN
Dreiländereck

GERMANY

DÜSSELDORF

Erkelenz
Hülcrath
Dormagen
Rhine
Gut Velderhof
Stommeln
COLOGNE
Jülich
Erft

HOL-
LAND

AUTOBAHN

Vijlen
AACHEN
Stolberg
Schevenhütte
Hauset
Hurtgen
Forest
Roetgen
Simonskall
Gut
Hombusch
Euskirchen
Mechernich
Eupen
Kall
Schleiden
Monschau

E I F E L

Elsenborn

BELGIUM

St. Vith

OPERATION CARNIVAL
March/April 1945

→ Flight approach of
the Werewolves

⇢ Escape route of
the survivors

*All territory to the West of the Rhine
was at this time in Allied hands.
(25 March 1945)*

0   5   miles   20
5   km   30

'WERE-WOLF: *a prehistoric WGmc compound whose constituents are represented by OE* wer *man and by OE* wulf *wolf; a person transformed into a wolf or capable of assuming a wolf's form.*'

WEBSTER'S NEW
COLLEGIATE DICTIONARY

'*Even if we could not conquer, we should drag half the world into destruction with us, and leave no one to triumph over Germany. . . . We may be destroyed, but if we are, we shall drag a world with us*—a world in flames!

JOSEF GOEBBELS, AUTUMN, 1934

INTRODUCTION

In the second half of the twentieth century we live in the age of the guerrilla.

If there are any heroes left in our time, they are the ragged, romantic, doomed young men and women who fight and die in the jungles of Central Africa, the deserts of the North, the teeming cities of Brazil and the slums of the American East Coast. Che Guevara, complete with beard and beret, stares down from a million teenage walls as the idol and icon of our time.

Once they were seen by the Establishment as the exponents of immature violence in an 'emerging' world. To-day we know that this is no longer the case. The guerrillas have come down from the hills and out of the jungles to prove just how vulnerable urban civilization really is. Once they discovered the value—in terms of publicity—of the hijacked airliner or the kidnapped foreign consul, they knew that the *real* battle for the public's hearts and minds was not to be fought in some obscure jungle or against some nameless authority. It was to be waged in the city and against a particular individual so that the murder of some hated police chief, for instance, would reap a crop of headlines all over the world. The *tupamaro* had arrived.

'To-day to be an assailant or terrorist is a quality that ennobles any honourable man', wrote Carlos Marighela,[1] the Brazilian urban guerrilla leader, going on to maintain that the urban guerrilla is sustained by moral superiority. He does not wait for orders. His duty is to act and not to retreat. '*It is better to act and be wrong than to do nothing!*'

For many this urban violence with its commitment to murder and mayhem is shockingly new, a sign of the degenerate times in which we

[1] Killed in Sao Paulo in 1970.

live. Yet there is nothing very new in the kidnapping or assassination of particular individuals to gain political advantage. In fact, one could say that the Governments of those urban western societies which to-day are so shocked by the events in Latin American countries, in Quebec, Belfast, Palestine, etc., started the whole sordid business some quarter of a century ago.

Indeed, one might make out a case for saying that it was the United Kingdom which began it all when it allowed the exiled Czech Government in London to drop two parachutists in their German-occupied homeland in December, 1941. These two men, Jan Kubis and Josef Gabcik, had as their mission the murder of the German overlord SS General Reinhard Heydrich, who ruled the occupied country from his palace in Prague, and whose efforts had convinced the ordinary man in the street to collaborate with the Germans. The two Czech officers carried out their task well enough. Heydrich was ambushed and murdered, and the enraged Germans retaliated with the notorious Lidice Massacre. Thereafter the Czechs and the Slovaks did not collaborate any more. The first urban guerrilla mission had been successful.

Naturally it was not only prominent military and political figures who were in danger of being kidnapped and murdered in Europe in those years in the 'cause of freedom'. During the Second World War, guerrilla movements sprang up all over the Continent. The *Maquis*, the *Union*, the *Chetniks*, *de Witte Armee*—these were just some of the many groups dedicated to fighting the German occupation forces by any conceivable means.

Yet surprisingly enough, Nazi Germany, the country which provoked these underground movements, never, itself, produced an effective guerrilla movement when it became clear that it was about to be occupied by the Allies. Hitler's Germany, committed to 'total war', never managed to organize a guerrilla force operating on the lines of the Polish rural underground or the French and Dutch resistance in the cities. When the war ended in May, 1945, the great majority of the German Army, who had so fanatically resisted the allied forces, surrendered their weapons and resigned themselves to defeat.

There was, however, a German plan for a resistance movement against the advancing Allies. In Berlin in November, 1944, the head of the SS, Heinrich Himmler, ordered the formation of a para-military guerrilla organization which would fight behind the Allied front, which had by then gained a footing in both the east and west of Germany. So was born the group known as *Unternehem Werwolf*—or the 'Werewolves', comprised of fanatical young Germans who still believed in the *Endsieg* or Final Victory.

This is the story of that short-lived Nazi guerrilla group, which, despite Dr Goebbels' boast that it 'would never surrender', disbanded ignominiously when Germany capitulated to the Allies on Luneburg Heath. The book describes for the first time the only successful mission carried out by the Werewolves, which took place in the spring of 1945, code-named, ironically, Operation Carnival.[1]

[1] Ironically, because in the Catholic German Rhineland, the spring months of February and March usually see the joyous, uninhibited celebration of the Lenten Carnival, which dates back to the Roman Feast of Bacchus.

I
The Drop

'You must have faith. *I still have ways and means of bringing the war to a victorious conclusion.*'

Adolf Hitler to SS General Kaltenbrunner, March 1945

The Fortress began to swing in from the North Sea, turning landwards towards the Belgian port of Antwerp. To try and deceive the enemy it began to lose height and as it did so the temperature went up. The second pilot unzipped the collar of his thick flying overalls, and glanced out of the window. There was not a light to be seen, however, for the Belgians were still observing the blackout strictly, although Antwerp had been in Allied hands for six months now.

Suddenly, the second pilot felt a dig in his ribs. It was his chief, who, with his free hand, pointed to his watch. The second pilot got to his feet and stumbled clumsily down the narrow corridor, past the navigator, to where the seven passengers were crouched in the corridor. Bending down to bring his mouth close to the Belgian's ear, the pilot bellowed above the roar of the engines: 'Fifteen minutes to Brussels!' The Belgian nodded in acknowledgement.

The Fortress began to pick up speed again, having completed its wide arc to avoid the city. Its four engines quickly brought it to its top speed of 325 mph. Ilse Hirsch, the only woman passenger, felt the metal at her back grow rapidly colder again. She shuddered and stared across the corridor at the Belgian. He was holding his reserve parachute tightly clasped to his stomach. Perhaps it was his first jump too. Anyway, he would be first to go when they reached Brussels. They had been together in the little hotel in the square opposite the railway station for almost two weeks before they had driven out to the airfield for the last time, yet she knew nothing about him. She knew only that he had to be engaged in the same undercover work as they were—all of them in that hotel had been. But unlike the rest of the 'guests' he had gone out of his way to avoid them, limiting himself to a terse 'good morning' or 'good night'.

They were nearing the target now and one of the sergeants from the belly guns began to work his way down the corridor, lurching from side to side with the bucking of the plane in the thick cloud. He stopped in front of the Belgian and without a word motioned to him to get up. For a moment the woman thought he might refuse to move, but he hesitated only a fraction of a second. Then he rose and followed the sergeant obediently to the door, where he positioned himself ready to jump, as they had been taught to do.

The Fortress began to slow down. They were over Brussels now. Earlier that evening they had come under flak, but the senior pilot took a chance. He switched on his position lights. Inside the plane the woman could see the reflection of the wing tip lights on the opposite wall. The ruse worked. There were none of those frightening lurches which had occurred when they came under fire an hour before. The Belgians or the British or whoever manned the guns below took the plane for one of their own.

The Sergeant had begun to unfasten the door. As he flung it open, an icy-cold blast of air swept in and the cabin was filled with the roar of the engines. The Belgian poised himself, ready to jump. The sergeant leaned forward and attached his 'chute line to the apparatus just above the door. Up ahead in the cockpit the second pilot was counting off the seconds. At the end of the count-down, the sergeant slapped the Belgian on the shoulder and the man leapt out into the darkness. The sergeant quickly closed the door after him and struggled with the catches. As he did so, the Fortress began to gather speed again.

Ilse Hirsch looked at her watch. It was nearly eleven. Soon they would be over the border where they were to jump. She looked across at the others. Lieutenant Wenzel, the leader of the group, had his eyes closed, but she knew that he was not asleep. His hand, which was clasped tightly around the pistol stuck in his leather belt, was white at the knuckles. She saw that Wenzel was scared. She glanced at Hennemann and Heidorn. The two guides stared straight into space, seemingly unaware of her interest. Next to them sat Morgenschweiss. The boy was only sixteen years old. Just before they had taken off, he had been his usual loud, boastful self, fussing with his pistol and dagger, as if he were going to do the 'job' all on his own. Now, for once he was silent; like Wenzel, he was afraid.

The only one who did not seem affected by what lay ahead of them was Leitgeb, their radio operator. He had taken off his flying helmet and his head was slumped forward in sleep. He was, thought Ilse Hirsch, the only real man in the group. Morgenschweiss was a silly boy, the two guides were professionals who would do what was expected of them, no more, no less. As for Wenzel, he still remained an enigma for her; she never knew what to make of him. She felt that Leitgeb was the only one she could rely on even though he had proved himself a terrible radio operator during the training exercises back at the castle. Feeling the need to rest, Ilse rested her head against the cold metal behind her and closed her eyes.

The Fortress was slowing down again. Again the sergeant made his way along the plane towards them and signalled that they should prepare themselves for the jump. Wenzel opened his eyes at once. Rising quickly, he went over to the door to supervise the dropping of their 'food bomb', as Morgenschweiss called the food container which was dropped just before they were.

Now they all got to their feet. Heidorn, who was to jump first, started back when the icy wind from the open door hit him in the face. The sergeant shouted something, but the wind snatched the words from his mouth. Heidorn looked over his shoulder and Hennemann, his companion, muttered angrily. The two men always stuck together, but nonetheless quarrelled frequently.

As they approached the dropping zone the pilot began to throttle back and the sergeant put his foot on the metal food container and turned to watch the other who, as before, was silently mouthing the countdown. As his mouth closed on zero, the sergeant booted the food container out of the door. Now it was Heidorn's turn. The NCO slapped him on the shoulder and, without hesitation, he launched himself into space, disappearing immediately into the night.

Hennemann followed. Then Wenzel. Morgenschweiss seemed to hesitate, and Ilse thought how pathetic he looked in his baggy cover-all. Then the sergeant's heavy hand slapped down on the boy's back and he vanished through the hatch, his hands grabbing instinctively for a support that was no longer there. The NCO turned and signalled to the woman. Obediently she walked across to him and almost without realizing it, with a push from his hand, she was out of the door and falling.

The wind howled about her ears and her breath was dragged forcibly from her. She felt herself falling at a crazy rate. Then with a clap like thunder and a great jerk that threatened to pull her arms from their sockets, the parachute opened. Abruptly her mad fall stopped, and she began to descend gently. As she swung slightly from side to side, she caught glimpses of the moonlit country beneath her. To one side there were hills, covered with rows of firs. To the other there was flat ground, on which lay patches of frozen snow. Reaching up carefully, she began to pull on the shroud lines as she had been taught at the airfield. It worked. The pendulum motion ceased. She was now coming down on the target area in a relatively straight line, heading for the thick forest on the heights to her left.

She had a few more moments to view her surroundings. As far as she could see, there was not a light or building to be seen, not even the dark lump of a farmhouse. The winter countryside seemed to be completely deserted. Naturally, she told herself, the curfew would keep the few remaining civilians in the area in their houses at this time of night. But what about the patrols? Anxiously she twisted her head and peered down, but she could see no one. Suddenly she wished she had not been so foolish as to refuse a pistol at the base. The others were all armed. She was the only one without a weapon. But there was no time to worry about that now. The ground was beginning to loom up larger and larger. The wider landscape had disappeared. She was landing on the heights. Resisting the urge to tense her body, she relaxed and, just before she hit the ground, clapped her legs together as she had been taught. Suddenly with a crash she was down. The branches of the firs broke her fall and she hardly felt the impact as she hit the ground. All the same she was winded and for a moment she lay there, swamped by her parachute, fighting for breath. There was no sound save that of her own breathing and the faint rustle of the firs. She was completely on her own. The mission had begun.

Hastily, she scattered some branches over her rolled-up parachute, then examined her work with the aid of the flashlight she wore on the breast of her coveralls. It was not perfect, but it would do. She kicked a few more leaves over the branches and shone the thin blue light on her wrist watch. It was just after eleven o'clock. On time. So far everything was running according to plan. But where was she? And more important, where were the others?

She turned her head to one side and tried to catch some small sound which might indicate where the others were. But all she could hear was the faint moan of the wind in the tree-tops and a very long way away the persistent rumble of the heavy guns, the ever-present background music of the war to which she had become so accustomed in these last six months.

She sucked in her breath and made a decision. She would have to move on. She could not simply wait there till some *Ami*[1] patrol caught her. Clambering up the nearest bank by what looked like an animal track, she began to walk slowly through the wood, flashing her torch every ten seconds. She left it on to the count of three and then switched off again. She did not want to attract the attention of enemy patrols, though she knew that the fighting troops were already a long way off on the Rhine. Perhaps even over it by this time The enemy troops left in this area were second-line men and

[1] German slang for 'American'.

second-line men were not usually inclined to carry out patrols in the thick of the forest at this time of night.

She must have walked for a good ten minutes before she caught the glimpse of an answering blue light. For a moment she did not trust her own eyes. But there it was! On and off and on again. She did not dare shout, but keeping her light on, she hurried breathlessly towards it. As she got closer, she saw to her relief other blue lights flickering off and on.

A few moments later she found the group. Wenzel, who was closest, gripped her arm and whispered as if the nearest enemy soldier was behind the next tree, 'Good, Ilse, you made it!'.

'Yes', she answered unnecessarily and saw quickly that all the others were present too.

'Let's find the container,' Wenzel said.

With their blue lights on and pistols at the ready, save for Ilse and Hennemann, who had lost his during the drop, they spread out, combing the dark woods for the food container. Once something moved rapidly in the firs, perhaps a startled deer, and Ilse felt her heart jump alarmingly.

'Find out where we are yet?' she asked Heidorn at her side.

'No, not yet,' the guide answered, 'but we're somewhere near the border, I think'.

They blundered on through the dripping firs for what seemed a very long time. Ilse was alarmed at the noise they were making but the men didn't seem to care. Although they were probably in their own country (if the first pilot's calculations had been correct), it was still enemy-occupied territory and she had no illusions about what would happen to them if they were captured; they would be lined up against the nearest wall and shot.

Suddenly, they came upon the container lodged in a clump of trees. Following a curt order from Wenzel, they dragged it out swiftly and distributed the supplies it contained— pumpernickel bread, cans, chocolate, two bottles of water each—stowing them in their rucksacks. Heidorn began coughing as he worked and Ilse wondered whether he had recovered from the pneumonia he had in the hotel. 'Stop that damned cough-ing,' Wenzel snapped. Heidorn muttered something angrily under his breath, but he stopped coughing.

When the container was empty they set to work to hide it. This was important. Its size and shape would certainly betray them if they didn't get it buried before dawn. All of them worked together to scoop a shallow hole in the earth. When this was done they placed the container in it, kicking the loose earth over its top and scattering fir branches on top of the earth for good measure.

They rested for a moment or two after their job was completed, then Wenzel pointed to a dark clump of firs some fifty feet away. 'We'll bed down there for the rest of the night', he ordered, 'and move off as soon as it gets dark to-morrow.'

Josef Saive, or 'Jost' as most of his pals in the Dutch border police called him, swung his English Mark IV rifle over his shoulder and went out of the Wolfhaag Border Crossing Post into the cold night air. 'Come back for a break and a coffee at midnight, Jost,' Sgt Hubert Finders, his chief, called after him.

'Thanks Sergeant,' he said over his shoulder.

'And don't forget, Jost,' Finders added, 'don't go into the woods alone.'

'Yes, Sergeant,' the young man answered dutifully.

He knew that the Sergeant meant well, but he seemed to think that enemy saboteurs were hiding behind every bush and tree in the thick woods that surrounded the little white-washed border post. Ever since the *Amis* had told them there was a danger the Germans might attempt to sabotage the bridge and tunnel down below in the valley on the Belgian side of the *Dreiländereck*,[1] Sgt Finders had insisted none of the police should go into the woods alone. Of course, Saive realized, the bridge and tunnel were important since *Amis* used them as their main rail supply-line to the front, but, he told himself, the Germans were just about finished. The only people who

[1] Literally 'Three country corner'.

occasionally tried to get across this part of the frontier illegally were smugglers; and on a bright moonlit night like to-night they would be hardly likely to make the attempt.

Wolfhaag Border Crossing was located in the *Dreiländereck*, a heavily wooded group of hills, which ran through Belgium, Holland and Germany. Now that fighting had stopped in the area, the *Dreiländereck* had resumed its traditional role as the ideal spot for smuggling goods back and forth across the various borders, especially into occupied Germany where the remaining inhabitants were only too happy to trade their watches and rings for Belgian cigarettes and Dutch coffee.[1]

Josef Saive, who came from the German-speaking Dutch village of Viljen, knew all about smuggling. Indeed more than one of his relatives had done a little part-time smuggling themselves when they had been laid off from the mines which studded the area. But in spite of the smuggling tradition of the border area, Josef had joined the Border Police as soon as it was re-established by the *Amis* in September, 1944, when they liberated that part of Holland. He would have liked to have joined the Army, but his mother had been against it. So he had to content himself with the Police. As least he had a smart US uniform with a bright yellow Dutch lion on his sleeve and an English rifle. Mlle Straat, the Belgian girl from the village of Gemmenich just across the border from Wolfhaag, was suitably impressed.

By the red-and-white-striped border pole a fellow policeman was talking to a Belgian civilian. 'Pigeons,' Josef said to himself, as he hitched his rifle more comfortably on his shoulder, 'I bet they're talking about pigeons.' They were.

'Evening,' he said to his colleague.

'Evening, Jost,' the policeman replied without looking

[1] In the immediate post-war years this twenty-square-mile area became the centre of professional gangs who smuggled into Germany. They resorted to all sorts of tricks to get their wares across the border, including the use of armoured cars bought as war surplus in Belgium and specially-trained dogs which carried contraband packs strapped to their bodies.

round. He was fanatically interested in racing pigeons, although everyone knew the *Amis* had forbidden anyone to fly pigeons in the border area because of their use in espionage.

Saive grinned to himself. 'Listen,' he said, 'you carry on talking about your pigeons, if you want. I'll just pop up to Post Four and see that everything's all right.'

The other policeman turned. 'Alone, Jost?,' he queried. 'You know what he said,' he indicated the border post with a jerk of his head. 'Don't worry. I'll only be a few minutes,' and hitching up his rifle once more, he hurried into the woods, striding effortlessly up the steep muddy trail that led to Post Four; at the crossroads formed by the logging trails in the woods, Mlle Straat from Gemmenich had promised to meet him for half an hour. Jost Saive, miner's son from Viljen, hurried on to his appointment with death at the hands of another miner's son, born less than twenty miles away.

Wenzel and Hennemann had argued about whether they were in Belgian or Dutch territory, but in the end Wenzel made the decision and set their direction. The officer seemed to know the area well enough although Hennemann and Heidorn who had served on this frontier for years were supposed to be the experts.

They set off in single file with Hennemann in the lead and Ilse bringing up the rear, tramping steadily uphill, avoiding the logging trails, sticking to animal tracks and footpaths. They skirted a ruined railway bridge which spanned the valley in which, unknown to them, lay the village of Gemmenich. As the light faded, the going became tougher and every now and again someone would trip and curse. Morgenschweiss, in particular, hampered by his overlarge *Ami* rubber boots, fell frequently and twice Wenzel snapped at him angrily to be more careful. In spite of the tough going, they all knew they had to be in their next hiding place above Aachen before dawn. The danger of moving once it became light was too great, especially as they were getting very close to the city.

After about an hour they came to the part of the border where Hennemann was to hide the dollars for the English agent. Now in the half-light, they could see everywhere the traces of the previous autumn's fighting; rusty abandoned equipment, helmets, gas-masks, coats, old cans of food, with here and there a burned-out tank hulk or a shattered cannon.

When they reached the place where it had been agreed they should hide the money, Hennemann, who was leading the group, came to a halt. Wenzel flicked on his torch. Its thin, blue ray illuminated a weathered border stone with a deep 'N' surmounted with a crown engraved on it. 'There,' he said to Hennemann, 'will that do?'

'Yes,' the guide answered softly. Kneeling in the light of the torch, he began to dig at the base of the stone with his knife. Ilse watched with interest, as he cleared a little hole and placed the yellow waterproof packet inside it. There was a small fortune in dollars in the package. Once they had completed their mission, the position of the money would be radioed to a British captain in their service. In due course, he would collect it as payment for his treachery to his country.

Grunting a little with the effort Hennemann shoved the soil back with his boot and then stamped it down hard. Morgenschweiss broke off a few twigs while Heidorn collected a pile of fir fronds. Together they scattered them over the freshly disturbed soil. Wenzel bent down to inspect their work and said, 'All right, let's get on. Time's passing and we've a lot to do tonight!' And in extended Indian file the group set off once more along their route.

Josef Saive had just looked at the luminous dial of his wristwatch; it was nearly twenty minutes since he had left the border post when he suddenly saw the Werewolves. They were directly to his front, spread out in single file as they swung round the bend in the trail. *Enemy saboteurs*! Hastily he unslung his rifle and whispered to Mlle Straat, 'Go back and get help!'

'What is—?' the words ended abruptly, as she followed the direction of his gaze.

'Don't talk,' Jost urged her. 'Go and get help. Run!'

The girl needed no urging now. Swiftly she turned and began to run through the trees the way she had come. Just before she vanished around the bend, she threw a quick glance over her shoulder. She could just make out Jost crouching behind a tree, his rifle at the ready. Then, panic-stricken, she ran towards the border post.

Jost Saive did not hesitate. As Sgt Finders observed later, 'Jost was a keen boy. He had visions of glory. He wanted action.' Licking his lips, which had suddenly become very dry, he cried out 'Hands up!'[1] The dark figures on the trail opposite him froze. But they didn't put their hands up.

Jost levelled his rifle, feeling the butt hard against his shoulder. 'Hands up,' he called again.

'Patrol!' Wenzel hissed, tugging at his pistol holster.

There was panic among the group as they fumbled frantically for their weapons. Surprisingly, it was Morgenschweiss who fired first. Drawing his pistol, he fired and flung himself simultaneously down the bank to his right.

The shot broke the spell. Jost pressed his trigger almost automatically. He fired again. Then the bullets started to cut the air all around him, smacking into the leaves and branches over his head. The first bullet that hit him caught him in the groin and he sank, doubled-up, to the ground.

As Saive fell, Ilse Hirsch rolled down the embankment to her left. She was surprised at Morgenschweiss's quick reactions; she had not thought the effiminate-looking youth had it in him. Then she was on her feet, running headlong through the dark wood, oblivious of the branches ripping at her face. By the time the firing died away, she was far from the scene of the fight.

Sgt Finders reacted immediately when he heard the shots. Stabbing out his cigarette, he grabbed his hat and pistol and shouted to the policeman standing by the barrier, 'Stay here and cover me, but don't come into the wood.' The man raised

[1] Why he should have called out in English no one has ever been able to find out.

his rifle instinctively. 'Look,' he cried. Someone was running down the trail from the wood.

'*It's me* . . . *Straat*!'

The soldier lowered his rifle. He recognized the Belgian girl. Finders sprang forward. 'What is it? What's going on,' he demanded.

'It's Jost,' the girl wept, 'spotted some saboteurs in—'

Finders did not allow her to finish the sentence.

'How many?' he snapped.

'I don't know . . . perhaps eight.'

Finders was no fool. He knew he had no chance with his pistol against eight men, but he could not let young Saive fight it out alone in the woods. He turned to the policeman. 'Get the Belgians!'—he meant the Belgian border guards at their post at the bottom of the hill—'and then follow me in'.

His heart thumping, Finders hurried up the steep trail. He soon found Jost. The boy was lying to the right of the path some 1,500 metres from the border post. He was paralysed from the waist downwards and moaning with pain. Anxiously Finders bent down and suddenly caught sight of the blood which was pouring from under his jacket.

Jost grabbed at him so wildly that he could not move. 'There were seven of them,' he cried hysterically. 'I shouted "Hands up".' He swallowed hard and fought for breath. Finders took stock of his wounds. The boy had been shot at close range in three places, but the worst wound was the one in his groin.

'And then what happened?' the Sergeant asked softly.

'When they didn't answer my challenge, I . . . I fired and they let loose with a machine pistol . . . They were Germans . . . Sergeant,' his voice changed suddenly, 'can you say the Act of Contrition with me? I'm going to die.'

'Of course you're not, Jost,' the NCO mumbled, but already the boy was beginning to rattle off the prayer, his fingers biting painfully into Finders' upper arm.

Reluctantly he joined in and then suddenly he became aware of the shapes emerging from the trees all about him. He felt the hair at the nape of his neck stand up. There were four of them. In the moonlight he could make out their silhouettes quite easily. But the boy hadn't seen them. He kept on rattling off the prayer in his native dialect,[1] his Dutch forgotten altogether in his moment of agony.

The figures remained where they were for what seemed an eternity to Finders, but what must have been, in fact, only a matter of a few seconds at the most. Then, as suddenly as they had appeared, they vanished into the bushes, grey and sinister, disappearing as silently as they had come.

Sgt Finders carried the dying boy back to the post and while the other policeman tried in vain to stop the flow of blood, he called for the doctor from nearby Vaals. It was a quarter of an hour before the doctor was able to come, but he got down to business at once. Jost's face was deathly pale and there was a blue colouring under his eyes which had not been there when they had carried him into the post.

When he had completed his examination, the doctor without a word went across to the bowl on the stove to wash his hands which were covered with blood. Finders looked at him anxiously. 'Is he going to be all right doctor?,' he queried.

'He's been hit in the left knee, right breast and groin. No, he's going to die.'

Finders' face contorted. 'If I'd only got him out of the wood quicker,' he groaned.

The doctor shook his head. 'It wouldn't have helped,' he said.

At 2145 precisely that night (Sgt Finders was a stickler for precision even at such moments as this and he noted the time in the official notebook) *Soldat* Josef Saive died of his wounds in the little frontier post at Wolfhaag. *Operation Carnival* had claimed its first victim.

Ilse Hirsch had kept moving all through the night. It was not until daybreak that she felt she was safe. Her flight had carried

[1] The border people speak a form of low German dialect as their native language.

her to the edge of the forest, near to their objective. Behind her there was no sound of pursuit and for a few minutes she rested weakly against the nearest tree. Then the mooing of a cow in a nearby field awoke her once more to the danger of her position. Where there were cows, there were farmers. She had to move—and move quickly!

Swiftly she bent down and unzipped the coverall. Beneath it she was dressed in a skirt and blouse. She shivered in the cold morning air. Throwing the camouflaged coverall in the nearest clump of bushes, she strode stiffly to the edge of the trees. Before her lay the fields, still covered with an early morning mist, running down steeply from the woods to the first ruined houses and then on to the city itself.

It was Aachen. Despite the mist, she could make out the damaged spires of the Dom.[1] There had been enough happy times before the war when, as an apprentice with the old bookseller, she had visited the ancient city on shopping sprees or with the BDM.[2] Now the city lay in enemy hands and this time her visit would be very different. Somewhere in the city was the man—she did not know his name yet—whom *Werwolf* had come to kill.

She slung her rucksack over her shoulder once more and set off across the fields towards the city from which she had fled so hastily six months before.

[1] The Cathedral.
[2] A German youth organization.—The Union of German Maidens, known as the 'Hitler Maidens'.

II
The Victim

'Somewhere or other there is already a para-trooper assigned to the job of murdering me.'

Chief Burgomaster Oppenhoff of
Aachen to his wife. February, 1945

I

On the afternoon of 5 September, 1944, General Eisenhower sat with his injured leg propped on a chair and scowled at the grey-green water of the English Channel. A couple of days earlier his little unarmed scout plane had force-landed on the beach near Granville, his Normandy headquarters, and in helping the pilot to push it through the wet sand before the tide turned, he had twisted his knee. As a result, to his great annoyance, the Supreme Commander found himself immobilized at his modest seaside headquarters, which bore the apt name of 'Villa Montgomery'. There was a great deal of work to be done but his injured knee confined him to his office. The famous ear-to-ear grin was noticeably absent.

Nor could this have happened at a worse time, for the campaign had reached a critical stage. That autumn his armies had been victorious in every sector. In August, they had broken out of their landing area in Normandy and swept rapidly through Brittany, past Paris, driving deep into Belgium and the southern part of Holland. Now because of the lack of good supply ports in allied hands, there was a shortage of fuel and ammunition, which had temporarily slowed up the advance. With his armies temporarily halted in northern France and Belgium, at most a day's march from the German frontier, Eisenhower knew he had to act quickly and decide what should be done next. It was a vital decision which could well bring about the last battle that would break the Germans for good.

Having made up his mind, Eisenhower dictated his orders for the forthcoming campaign, pausing only to light another of the forty-odd cigarettes he smoked a day. 'For some days,' he said, 'it has been obvious that our military forces can advance almost at will, subject only to the requirements for maintenance. Resistance has largely melted all along the front. From the beginning of this campaign I have always envisaged that as soon as substantial destruction of the enemy forces in France could be accomplished we should advance rapidly on the Rhine by pushing through the Aachen Gap in the north and through the Metz Gap in the south. The virtue of this movement is that it takes advantage of all existing lines of communication in the advance towards Germany and brings the southern force on the Rhine at Coblentz, practically on the flank of the forces that would advance straight through Aachen. I see no reason to change this conception.'

The attack on Aachen, the first German city in the path of the advancing Americans and the first German city to be attacked by land in a century, was on.

At his headquarters near the Belgian city of Verviers, General Courtney Hodges, the commander of the US First Army welcomed the Eisenhower directive to take Aachen. Hodges was determined to gain some acclaim for himself and his Army. It seemed to him that throughout the Normandy campaign the First Army had been doing most of the fighting and as a result had suffered heavy casualties. Yet, 'Blood and Guts' Patton,[1] who commanded the Third Army, despite the fact he had faced lighter opposition and had incurred fewer casualties, had been able, with his flair for publicity, to capture the head-lines. Now with Patton bogged down in front of the city of Metz with no likelihood that it would fall in the near future, Hodges felt that the capture of Aachen, the first German city of any consequence, would give him and his hard-pressed men the publicity they felt they had earned. Nonetheless, he knew that the capture of the gateway into Germany would be no walk-over. American intelligence had been able to tell him enough about Aachen to make him realize that the city would be a tough nut to crack.

The fortifications round Aachen were part of the Siegfried Line defences which ran from the Dutch frontier to the Swiss border. They presented a formidable barrier consisting of deep belts of elaborately interconnected pillboxes and bunkers,

[1] One cynical GI in Patton's Army is reported to have wisecracked, '*Yeah, our blood and his guts!*'

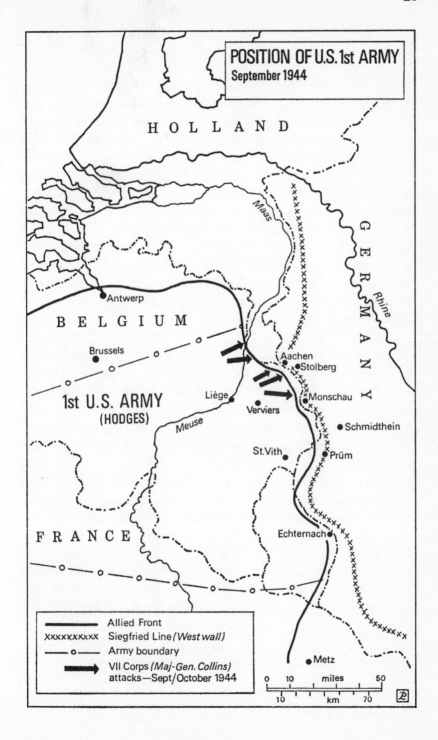

POSITION OF U.S. 1st ARMY
September 1944

HOLLAND

Maas

GERMANY

Rhine

Antwerp

BELGIUM

Brussels

Aachen
Stolberg

1st U.S. ARMY
(HODGES)

Liège

Monschau

Verviers

Schmidthein

Meuse

St.Vith

Prüm

FRANCE

Echternach

Metz

Allied Front
xxxxxxxxxx Siegfried Line *(West wall)*
—o— Army boundary
VII Corps *(Maj-Gen. Collins)*
attacks—Sept/October 1944

0   10   miles   50
10   km   70

some of them with eight-foot-thick, ferro-concrete walls, shielded with steel plates. Along natural defence lines such as the Rhine, the Siegfried fortifications were less elaborate, but in the vulnerable Moselle valley and, above all, in the Aachen plain there were pillboxes zig-zagging through the countryside to a depth of twelve miles. Moreover, there was a second defensive line running parallel to the frontier. And even if that were penetrated, the approach to the city itself was blocked by a maze of coal-mines in the surrounding hills which could easily swallow up division after division of infantry, making air and armoured superiority of little use to the advancing forces.

There was little doubt that the Germans intended to make a stand at Aachen. Goebbels, the Nazi Minister of Propaganda, was already thumping the big drum, saying that the city would be another Stalingrad for the Americans and that they would never take the 'Holy Imperial City where for six hundred years German emperors had reigned'.

Hodges decided to surprise the city with a swift armoured thrust, hoping that with luck he might 'bounce' through the defences before the Germans had a chance to reinforce their troops with the enemy divisions that had retreated in disorder from Belgium. He gave the job of breaching the defences around Aachen to the US VII Corps and its commander 'Lightning Joe' Collins.

General Hodges relied heavily on the commander of VII Corps. While Corlett of XIX Corps was a sick man and Gerow of V was modest and a little pedestrian, like Hodges himself, Major-General Joe Collins was an aggressive commander who, despite his youthful 'all-American boy' appearance, had fought in France in World War One. He had gained himself the nickname 'Lightning Joe' by his flamboyant handling of the 25th (Lightning) Infantry Division at Guadalcanal. His reputation for bold leadership had been enhanced by his conduct of the siege and capture of Cherbourg in July, 1944.[1]

---

[1] Collins was also Montgomery's favourite corps commander among the Americans; during the Battle of the Bulge in December, 1944, he asked for him specifically to command the US counter-attack.

At this time, Collins had two veteran infantry divisions under his command, the 1st and 9th, both of which had been in action since the North African campaign of 1942,[1] and the 3rd Armoured Division, one of only three armoured units in the American Army which had remained at full strength. Yet, despite the experience of the men under his command, Collins was not altogether happy with his new assignment. He realized that the capture of Aachen was no easy task, yet he agreed with Hodges that he might be able to 'bounce' his way through the defences before the Germans dug-in in any force. He began plans for the armoured thrust at once.

On 10 September, the corps artillery of the VII Corps took up its position in an orchard just on the Belgian side of the frontier and started pounding the area round Aachen. That same day the reconnaissance company of the 33rd Armoured Regiment, led by Colonel Welborn, captured the small German town of Roetgen and thus became the first invader since the time of Napoleon to occupy German territory. On the eleventh, the same division moved up into the shadow of the Siegfried Line and started blasting its way into the frontier town of Stolberg, five miles to the west of Aachen, with the rest of the division strung out over Holland, Belgium and France. On its flank the 1st Infantry Division kept pace with it and so effective was the advance that, as the day drew on, the Americans in the surrounding hills could see the dim silhouette of Aachen itself.

But later that day the advance came to a sudden halt. Supplies were running out. Hodges realized that he could not supply Collins with the necessary ammunition for the projected five-day battle until the fifteenth. As a result, in spite of Collins' energetic protests, Hodges ordered him to halt his drive forward for at least two days.

While the Americans hung back, the Germans acted. Throughout the night of 11 September, confusion and fear had reigned at German Seventh Army headquarters which had charge

[1] At this time they were probably the most experienced and capable infantry formations in the whole US Army.

of the Aachen sector. But when it became clear, on the morning of the 12th, that the American advance had stopped and that they were confining themselves to reconnaissance sorties, the commanding general, *General der Panzertruppen*[1] Erich Brandenberger began to take heart. He knew only too well that his position was very serious. To cover the Aachen Gap he had only the 81st Corps under General Friedrich-August Schack, made up of four badly mauled divisions, two of them infantry and two of them armoured, the once proud 9th and 116th Panzer Divisions.

During the lull, the evacuation of Aachen's remaining sixty thousand civilians was resumed so that the city's defence would not be hampered by the extra mouths to feed, and General von Schwerin, commander of the 116th Panzer Division, which was still regrouping north of Aachen, was ordered into the city itself to take over its defence.

Von Schwerin arrived in Aachen late on the night of the twelfth, his Army *Volkswagen* fighting its way through the panic-stricken Aacheners, fleeing from the city which was already burning from the first American shells. All civilian administration in the city had come to a halt. All trains had stopped running at midnight. The local Nazi party leaders who a few days before had so eagerly echoed Goebbels' claim that 'no enemy foot would ever enter Aachen' had 'evacuated' themselves to the town of Jülich some twenty miles away.

The big General smiled ironically. 'I suppose that's far enough', he murmured. Goebbels had claimed that Aachen, the old Imperial German city, would be defended by selected élite troops. 'Our enemies will break their teeth on Aachen'. 'Elite troops', the General mused cynically. Christmas soldiers, he called them, old men and untrained boys. 'How many civilians are there still in the city?' he asked the colonel in charge of the HQ at the Hotel Quellenhof. 'It's hard to say, sir. Perhaps forty thousand.'

'All right. Make a public announcement that I, as battle

[1] Tank Corps General.

commandant of Aachen, order that there will be no further attempt to evacuate the city. I believe that the Senior Burgo-master[1] left an emergency administration behind. I want those people to report to me at once.'

Von Schwerin soon made it clear to both his officers and the remaining members of the city administration that he felt any defence of Aachen was senseless. The city had already experienced over five hundred air raids and was over fifty per cent destroyed. Now, with his own weak 116th Panzer Division outnumbered by at least three to one it was being bombarded by enemy aircraft and artillery. On the 14th, he had posters placed all over the city which proclaimed 'If the town is taken by the enemy, avoid any individual action against them. Don't forget that you are Germans! Keep your honour as Germans! But avoid any action which would give the enemy cause to take reprisals.' That same day he took a step which sealed his own fate. While the American artillery pounded the city, he wrote a letter to the commander of the enemy troops. It read:

'I stopped the absurd evacuation of this town—therefore, I am responsible for the fate of its inhabitants and I ask you to take care of the unfortunate population in a humane way. I am the last German Commanding Officer in the sector of Aachen.'

(signed) Schwerin.

The General then summoned an official of the postal service. 'I've asked you to come here because I have a task for you upon which depends the future of your home town. I have a communication here which I want you to give to the first American officer who enters your office if the city is taken. Ask him to give it to his commanding officer at once. This letter will be decisive for the future of the local population. Do

[1] This was Senior Burgomaster Janssen who had ordered the original evacuation at the command of the Gauleiter of Cologne. He had then left the city himself and gone to Siegen, some hundred miles away on the other side of the Rhine.

you realize your responsibility?' The man nodded and von Schwerin dismissed him. Now there was nothing else he could do but wait for the arrival of the Americans; he felt he had saved the ancient city.

While this was going on, General Collins was still waiting for authority to renew the attack. Meanwhile he determined to execute what he called a 'reconnaissance in force'. The First Division was ordered to swing south of the city after breaking through the first pillbox belt, while the Third Armoured Division was commanded to push forward up the Stolberg corridor.

The Big Red One, as the division was known because of its insignia, went into the attack with all the confidence of its many years of experience. But even the most battle-hardened of the troops were shaken when they cleared the hills and saw the Siegfried Line stretching before them, five rows deep of gleaming concrete blocks of uneven shape and size, calculated to make a tank throw a track or expose its unarmoured belly when it crossed them. The bright white concrete 'dragon's teeth' extended across the valley until one end disappeared into a distant wood and the other over the horizon. In front of the 'dragon's teeth' ran a ditch, some 15 feet deep and broad, and in front of that barbed wire entanglements interspersed with minefields. And the first flat crack of an 88 mm told the advancing infantry that somewhere in the hills behind these first defences there were pillboxes armed with heavy artillery.

But it was the 3rd Armoured's tanks which were the first to test the strength of the defences around Aachen. Led by General Maurice Rose[1] a command unit of the division advanced right into the Siegfried line itself. In the van Task Force X commanded by Lt-Col Leander Doan, comprising two battalions, one infantry and one armoured, plus a platoon of engineers, moved steadily forward despite heavy fire. In the face of intense machine gun fire, the two groups pushed

[1] Killed in a German ambush in the last few weeks of the war, while leading his division in the Ruhr Pocket.

through the first tank barrier up to the first crest from where they could see the dragon's teeth. Here a bitter exchange of fire took place but the Americans found it impossible to knock out the German artillery. Nevertheless they were still able to struggle forward, the engineers sweating under their heavy demolition charges. Yard by yard they got closer to the concrete line. Suddenly a pillbox, which the Americans thought had been knocked out, came to life again and started spraying the first line of infantry with Spandau fire. Under Capt Bill Plummer, a platoon rushed it from both sides. In spite of their casualties they got within range of it. Just before he ordered the engineers to explode their tetrayl satchel charges which would send the pillbox skyhigh, Capt Plummer crouched on the 'blind side' of the Germans and called 'Come and out and surrender!'

For a moment there was no reply.

'*Raus*!' he repeated.

'Go to hell,' a voice said in English from within the pillbox.

Plummer nodded to the corporal.

The next moment the pillbox and its defenders disappeared in a cloud of smoke.

Midday came and still Col Leander Doan's tanks were unable to break through. Then the Americans had a lucky break. Someone found a cart track which had apparently been built by the local farmers so that their carts could cross the dragon's teeth. Col Doan was quick to seize his opportunity. He realized, however, that the track might be mined, so he sent in a Scorpion flail tank to check that the track was clear.

The Tank Commander, Sgt Dahl, drove down the narrow track in low gear, the chains of his tank flailing the earth in front of him to explode any teller mines buried on the path— but the track was not mined. Just as he was congratulating himself on the success of the mission, the Scorpion came to an abrupt halt. For a moment he thought he had been hit. Then, cautiously opening the hatch, he peered out. The cause of the abrupt stop was not hard to find. By a hundred to one chance, one of the chains had caught on the spike of the first row of dragon's teeth. Swiftly he rapped out an order to his driver and the Corporal reversed, but with all the power at their disposal it was impossible to drag the tank away from the dragon's tooth.

Just that moment the German artillery discovered the trapped Scorpion and the 88 mm opened up with a vengeance. Dahl did not hesitate. Unplugging his mike hurriedly, he cried 'Let's get the hell out of here!' Together he and his crew pelted to the rear with the German shells exploding all around them.

In spite of the mishap Col Doan was determined to make use of the track. Together with Lt John Hoffmann, and Sgt Dahl, he braved the enemy fire to return to the trapped Scorpion. Once there, they fixed steel hawsers to it and to two Shermans so that they could pull it free and unblock the passage. Dahl himself took the Scorpion's controls and after some manoeuvring they managed to clear the track.

Although by now the light was beginning to go, Doan did not hesitate. He slipped some twenty Shermans past the Scorpion, but the Germans were waiting for them. Enemy soldiers popped up from trenches on both sides of the track. There was a sharp crack and a shower of fiery red sparks that indicated a German *panzerfaust*.[1] Within the space of a few minutes, four of Doan's tanks were hit and came to an abrupt halt, thick blue smoke pouring from their engines. The crews flung themselves to safety, knowing from experience how easily the Shermans went up in flames.

Nor did the American punishment end there. A battery of assault guns which had been unloaded from Aachen trainsidings only a few hours earlier suddenly opened up at the advancing tanks. The huge lumbering Ferdinands made short work of the thinly-armoured and outgunned Shermans. Within a quarter of an hour Colonel Doan lost a further six tanks and by nightfall he had only ten tanks left. Doan ordered the attack to halt. Aachen would not fall to the Americans that day.

[1] A kind of one-shot bazooka.

When the news reached General von Schwerin that the Americans had halted, he knew that his life hung on a thread. Since the attempt on his life on 20 July, Hitler passionately hated his professional Wehrmacht generals and now by halting the evacuation of Aachen he had ignored an order which had originated with the Fuehrer himself. Von Schwerin knew that it was tantamount to a death sentence to disobey Hitler and be caught doing so.

On 15 September, the party officials began to crawl back into the city. At five o'clock that morning Dr Cremer, the deputy head of the emergency city administration, was arrested while still in bed. Sometime later the whole of the administration was similarly arrested and taken to nearby Würseten for questioning by the Gestapo. The next day, General von Schwerin learned that his letter had fallen into the hands of the Gestapo. Later in the morning, he received a written order instructing him to give up his post as battle commandant of Aachen. He was being replaced and he knew what that meant. Gathering about him soldiers of his divisional reconnaissance regiment, many of whom came from the Rhineland and were reluctant to see Aachen or any part of their homeland turned into a battlefield, he fled to a farmhouse near Aachen and dug in behind a screen of heavy machine guns. Here he decided to wait until Aachen fell and the war ended.[1]

Meanwhile a special unit of the Berlin SA under command of a Major Zimmermann had entered the beleagured city. This group of old party men who had been fanatical supporters of Hitler from the very start had no time for softness or weakness. On the afternoon of his arrival, Major Zimmermann ordered the evacuation of all civilians to re-commence. In a public announcement, he commanded 'only those may remain in

[1] General von Schwerin, from whose ancestral landholdings the original cadre of the 116th Panzer had come, kept his head, thanks to his influence with such officers as Field Marshals Model and Rundstedt, but he lost command of his beloved division.

Aachen who have a place in the coming battle. Everything else is ballast. Everything else must be removed without mercy.'

At the same time a new battle commandant for Aachen was instated; Oberst (Colonel) Wilck was determined to carry out the Fuehrer's orders to fight to the last man and the last bullet. Wilck appointed as his second-in-command in charge of the city itself Colonel Leyherr, CO of the 689th Grenadier Regiment, who set up his headquarters in the Hotel Quellenhof. Together these two men and the representatives of the Party who had remained in the city set about organizing it for the battle to come.

While the two officers gathered together what soldiers they could, Zimmermann's men roamed the ruined and burning streets forcing the civilians from their homes, to join the long, sad lines leaving the city. If they resisted, Zimmermann's louts drew their pistols; and although the local population of Germany's most Catholic city had nothing but contempt for those heathen '*Goldfasanen*'[1] they had no alternative but to comply.

Ilse Hirsch was one of those who left during that second week of September. She did so hesitantly, not because she wanted to stay in Aachen until the *Amis* captured it, but because she longed to stay and fight. For six months she had lived and worked in the city, teaching its young girls their duty to Fatherland and Fuehrer, but she was not satisfied with her role as a teacher and organizer with the BDM. Now when her Fatherland was in dire need, she wanted to do something more active than teach youngsters the history of the Party. But there was no place for her in the defence of Aachen and she was told by her Party friends that she must leave with the rest. Obedient as ever, she let herself be persuaded, deciding to take the offer of a lift in a motor-cycle side-car to the nearby town of Monschau, where she had lived previously.

[1] A satirical name given to the party officials who during the war had added great golden decorations to their party uniforms, thus gaining the title 'golden pheasants'.

She was within a few kilometres of the little town when the motorcycle broke down. Cursing and fuming the driver crouched in the mud by the roadside trying to fix it, while the stream of refugees from Aachen flowed past them. But it was too late. Somewhere up ahead, voices began to shout, 'They're coming!. . . They're coming!' Ilse Hirsch peered impatiently up the length of column. 'Who's coming?' she asked. An old man turned and grinned at her. There was something malicious in the way he looked at her. 'The *Amis* of course, who did you think?' Ilse Hirsch and the rest of the column had bumped into General Craig's 9th Infantry Division advancing on Monschau as part of Collins' encirclement of Aachen. The Americans were in Monschau!

For a moment, Ilse Hirsch stood rooted to the spot. Then she acted. Seizing her rucksack from the back of the side-car, she slung it quickly over her back and ran into the woods, heedless of any mines that might have been buried there. The Americans were not going to catch her. She was certain of that.

II

Wilck and Collins were waiting to see who would make the next move. In the end the Germans moved first. While Collins prepared to open his attack on 17 September, German artillery began to pound the positions of the 16th Infantry Regiment of the 'Big Red One' at 0600 precisely. In well-disciplined waves, with bayonets fixed, a battalion of German infantry from the experienced 12th Division tried to break the contact between the 1st Division and Maurice Rose's Third Armoured Division.

The attackers ignored the fact that the Americans were well dug-in on a hill position. As soon as the last hollow echoing sound of the artillery barrage had died away, they started up the long treeless hill in sound skirmisher's fashion. A few men would run ahead, drop and begin to fire, allowing the next group to break cover and follow. Yard by yard they edged themselves up the hill. The veteran infantrymen of the 1st waited and held their fire.

When the Germans came within close range a ripple of rifle fire went down the line. A moment later the slower clack of a machine gun joined in. The first line of Germans vanished, flung aside as if struck down by some gigantic fist. The attackers hesitated for a moment and then came on again, shouting at the tops of their voices. Over their heads, their own artillery joined in again, trying to knock out the enemy positions. The American line held firm, however, and within an hour the German attack was broken. The hillside was littered with corpses. A wounded German was hauled in by American medics and as he puffed gratefully on a Lucky Strike he said to his captors, 'We've been three years on the Russian front and we have been beaten before. But this is the first time we have ever been stopped by small arms fire.'

An hour later another German battalion took up the attack. But like their predecessors they had forgotten they were still silhouetted against the sky in the poor autumn light. They made perfect targets for the American artillery and mortars. As a result, they were subjected to heavy fire as soon as they left their cover. Still they came, in ragged little groups, urged on by their young officers who sometimes wore caps to distinguish themselves from the helmeted soldiers and thus make themselves clearly identifiable to their men as rallying points. By mid-day, the German attack had come to a halt, with nearly half a regiment casualties suffered for the loss of twenty Americans.

Nor did the Germans have any better success against the 3rd Division south-east of Stolberg. Under the command of ambitious young Col Engel, who at thirty-six had won the Knight's Cross in Russia and then become one of Hitler's adjutants, the 12th German Division hit Combat Command B of the American 3rd Division in the former's first day in action in the Aachen sector. The Germans struck the Americans at mid-day just as the Americans were about to launch their own attack. The result was confusion and casualties, with neither side being able to make any progress.

Much the same thing occurred at Schevenhuette, where the Americans had made their deepest penetration of the Siegfried Line defences. Here, however, Colonel Smythe, commander of the 47th Infantry, decided to postpone his own scheduled attack till he was clear what the German intention was. Just after ten, one of his men, Staff-Sgt Harold Hellerich who was leading a fighting patrol, spotted a German infantry force moving across the open fields towards Schevenhuette. Immediately the Sergeant got on the radio-phone to his company commander. The latter immediately called for an artillery bombardment and while Hellerich and his men opened up and pinned the Germans to the ground, the artillerymen to the rear found the range of the enemy. Of the two hundred Germans in the attacking force only ten got away.

The Germans suffered heavy casualties throughout the day until, finally, Col Engel asked General Schack, his Corps Commander, for permission to call off his division's attack. Privately Schack thought Engel had handled his division badly on its first day under his command. The Fuehrer's favourite had launched his men too hurriedly in unco-ordinated piecemeal attacks so that his forces had been cut to pieces by the Americans. In a single day's combat, one of his battalions had been reduced to a fifth of its original strength. Schack was renowned for his blunt speaking, but for once he kept his opinion to himself. It was rumoured that Engel had been given the 12th Division for the defence of Aachen by Hitler himself. Schack, therefore, agreed to Col Engel's request and the German attacks on the 1st Infantry and the 3rd Armoured ceased.

But if 17 September was disastrous for the Germans, it had brought little encouragement to 'Lightning Joe' Collins. Though his men had held grimly to their positions everywhere, he knew only too well that there were no reserves to back up his drive for Aachen and that the 1st and 3rd Divisions would have to go it alone in completing their encirclement of the city. Meanwhile, it seemed that the Germans had somehow found some reserves. He had certainly not expected to find himself in such a sticky position at this stage of the game. He guessed ruefully that the easy pursuit of the Germans through France and Belgium had spoiled him a little; in these last weeks he had grown used to breaking through the German defences with little opposition. Now at Aachen it was clear that things were different; it was not merely a question of 'bouncing' his way through the first German city in the path of the Allied armies. The pursuit was over. The great slog was just beginning.

In the last week of September, the 1st Infantry Division recommenced its advance towards Aachen, opposed by battle groups from the German 9th Panzer Division. The German defences were well co-ordinated and stubborn, and the Americans were severely hampered by thick mud caused by the persistent rain. The fighting was savage indeed. Every house—and in some cases, every room of every house—was defended to the last, and American patrols suffered terrible losses wherever they crossed the German lines. Each time it looked as if the Americans might make some substantial gain, the Germans would launch a counter-attack and throw them back to their former positions.

American losses round Aachen, in the Hurtgen Forest and at Monschau (which was also in the First Army's sector), were mounting at an alarming rate. Realizing just how appalling the combat conditions were, General Huebner, commander of the First Army, determined to boost the morale of his dispirited men. He therefore singled out fifty officers and men and summoned them to his cottage headquarters. The exhausted men, having formed up in a double rank, waited in the pelting rain until the three generals, Hodges, Collins and Huebner, followed by their staff officers, emerged from their headquarters. The generals then paced solemnly up and down the ranks awarding each man a decoration for bravery; sixteen silver stars were handed out at this one ceremony. Meanwhile, the battle raged on.

But the high-ranking commanders were beginning to lose heart too. Although the First Army sent General Bradley, the overall commander of the 12th Army Group to which the First belonged, a bust of Hitler on which was inscribed the boast, 'Found in Nazi Headquarters, Eupen, Germany. With seven units of fire and one additional division, First U.S. Army will deliver the original in thirty days,' both Bradley and Eisenhower knew that Hodges was no longer so sanguine about the speedy capture of Aachen as he had been in early September. With the high casualty rate, many of the veterans in the First Army were being replaced with less experienced men.

The Germans were suffering too. As the Americans got closer to the city, their artillery bombardment became a permanent feature of daily life, so that soldiers and civilians were forced to live underground, emerging like rats, only when it grew dark. Under these frightful conditions, the will of the civilians to resist grew steadily weaker.

While General Collins prepared for his last major attack on the embattled city, a German patrol crept through the woods north of Monschau. Its task was to ascertain the strength of the American dispositions in that sector of the front. Some members of the patrol had served in this section of the line before the American attack and because of their excellent local knowledge and the nature of the terrain, which offered excellent cover, they managed to penetrate far behind the American line in search of information.

It was thus that they came across the lonely hunting lodge set deep in the fir forest overlooking the picturesque ruins of Monschau's medieval castle. Since they could see smoke emerging from a chimney they approached the wooden house with caution. As they got close to the building, one of their number advanced while the rest covered him in tense expectation.

Suddenly the door of the little wooden lodge opened and a woman emerged. When she saw the soldier crouched there in the middle of the clearing, his machine gun at the ready, her hand flew to her mouth and she froze rigid with fright. For a moment the two stood there facing each other and then the woman's hand dropped and she smiled with relief as she recognized their grey-green uniforms. '*Deutsche Soldaten!*' she cried.

The other members of the patrol began to emerge rather sheepishly from the forest, embarrassed that they had allowed themselves to be frightened by a woman—and a German to boot. Laughing and chattering they clumped into the little wooden house. Ilse Hirsch had been rescued; it was not long before she was once more safely behind the German lines.

III

On 2 October, 'Lightning Joe' Collins sprang his final assault on the City of Aachen. This time the First Infantry Division was to pound its way through the narrow zone still separating it from the 30th Infantry Division which was swinging round the other side of the city. Once this had been achieved, Aachen would be surrounded.

The First Infantry's attack was less than twenty-four hours old when the Germans counter-attacked. At mid-day on 3 October, the 27th German Infantry Division, supported by eight self-propelled heavy guns and 'Goliaths'[1] hit the American foxhole line after a murderous artillery barrage in which 3,500 shells landed on the American positions. A lucky shot blew the first Goliath sky-high and then the divisional artillery joined in and knocked out four of the German assault guns in quick succession. The enemy infantry wavered and broke. The 'Big Red One' pushed on.

Throughout that first bitterly cold week of October, the Americans battled their way nearer and nearer to the city which they could now see in the valley below through the smoke of the battle. Time and time again the Germans counter-attacked, desperately trying to stave off the inevitable. But

[1] A miniature, radio-controlled tank filled with high explosives.

Collins was not going to be thwarted once again. He ordered that the attack should be pressed home with all energy, in spite of mounting American casualties and shortage of heavy shells. On 10 October, he tried to bring the uneven battle to an end by sending Lt-Col William Boehme under a white flag to request Wilck to surrender, giving him twenty-four hours to decide; and to make sure the population knew that the Battle Commandant would be responsible for their further suffering if he *didn't* surrender, Collins ordered shells bearing the surrender ultimatum to be fired into the crippled city.

Oberst Wilck refused to see Boehme, and as the latter could not seem to find any responsible officials or officer with whom he could talk, he returned to his own lines and reported his lack of success directly to General Huebner who passed on the news to Collins. But the VII Corps Commander decided to give Wilck a chance to change his mind. The hours ticked by slowly. In Berlin, Hitler announced that Aachen would be defended to the last 'even if it is reduced to a heap of rubble'. They were prophetic words.

At precisely 10 o'clock, the American attack started with an unrivalled intensity and fury. The Americans had waited the twenty-four hours. Now Oberst Wilck was going to regret his pride. While the VII Corps artillery brought its full weight to bear on the city, three hundred planes launched a tremendous bombing attack. A thousand bombs landed on the target to be followed over the next 48 hours by some 5,000 heavy shells. Aachen disappeared in smoke, which the powerful glasses of waiting American observers high in the hills around the town could not penetrate for days. Now the Americans had to rely on the intercepted wireless reports of Wilck's own radioman crouched deep in the Oberst's bunker command post as he broadcast them to the High Command far away in Berlin.

'Tactical Time 9.30, 13 October. Enemy attack with ten tanks and 100 infantrymen down the Jülich Strasse towards the Elisabeth Kirche. Direction: Quellenhof . . .'

'Tactical time 10 o'clock. Command Post Wilck under direct tank fire . . .'

'Tactical Time 10.48. Staff fighting enemy tanks . . .'

'Tactical time 10.53. Up to now six enemy tanks destroyed in close combat . . .'

Then a long pause till 12.35.

'Enemy positions directly opposite Command Post. We are moving to the Salvator tunnels. Out . . .'

The murderous house-to-house fighting in the centre of the crippled city followed the same pattern each day. First a flight of Thunderbolts would carry out a low-level rocket attack. Then while the German defenders were still paralysed, the infantry would rush forward, dashing through the ruined walls. Supporting them there was always a tank destroyer which would rumble slowly down the scarred streets, its great long 90 mm gun swinging warily from side to side waiting for the opposition to show itself.

And it always did. The men of the SS Parachute Regiment, who were the backbone of the resistance within the city, never failed to recover from the dive-bombing in time to counter the attack. The unmistakable high-pitched burr of a Spandau machine gun would announce to the advancing GI's that there was still plenty of will to resist and within seconds the battle would be raging again; the tank destroyer invariably scuttling backwards down the ruined street, trying to escape before the German bazookamen commenced their suicide attacks. In that second week of October, gains were counted in yards, or more precisely, in houses.

But on 14 October, Collins finally managed to encircle the city. To mark the event, the senior commanders of the First Army were presented to King George VI who was visiting the front at Verviers. The celebration was held in the dining-room of the ruined château which stood near Hodges' tented head-quarters. As usual, Hodges did not manage to come out of his shell in spite of the victory his men had achieved and it was 'Blood and Guts' Patton who once again dominated the scene.

Sipping his black coffee and regaling the King with stories of the North African Arabs' thieving ways, he declared loudly, 'Why I must have shot a dozen Arabs myself!'

Eisenhower, as always tolerant of his flamboyant Third Army commander, looked at him and asked with a wink, 'How many did you say, George?' Patton pulled at the big cigar he was holding in the other hand, 'Well, maybe it was only a half a dozen'.

'How many?' Eisenhower asked again.

Patton hunched his shoulders, laughed and turned to the King, 'Well, at any rate, sir, I did boot two of them squarely in the -ah, street at Gafsa.'

While the generals celebrated, the battle in the streets of Aachen went on. By now it was entering its last phase, for the German defenders were weakening rapidly. The civilian population had had enough. Looting became widespread and drunkeness was almost universal as both soldiers and civilians began breaking into the city's huge spirit stores. The SS parachute battalion carried out its last demolitions in accordance with Hitler's scorched-earth command and then tried to break out of the encircled city. But they ran into American fire on every front and the handful of survivors were forced to fall back. They retreated house by house until, with their ammunition exhausted, they reached the Hotel Quellenhof, where, it was rumoured, there was ammunition in the cellar. With the Americans at their heels, they clattered down the steps. A grimy blood-stained soldier, his face black with powder burns, flung off the lid of the first case with his bayonet. It was filled with empty champagne bottles! So was the second and the third. Above them they could hear the Americans entering the hotel, firing as they came.

For a moment the SS paratroopers hesitated. Then seizing a bottle each, they stormed up the stairs and rushed the Americans. Momentarily, the Americans were shocked into inaction. Then the Germans were among them, striking heads and helmets with their empty bottles. The dark lobby of the old hotel became a blood bath. Only one or two of the fanatical para-troopers escaped.

By the 18th the Americans had penetrated to the very centre of the city, using flame throwers to fight their way into the square near the Cathedral that Charlemagne had built. In the cellar of the Geka department store they discovered the Bishop of Aachen, Dr van der Velden, hiding among dusty packing cases. He had refused to be evacuated and had hidden from Zimmermann's SA men. He was rushed to the commanding general of the 'Big Red One', and from him to the interrogating officers. It was probably on that day or the one following that he made his fatal recommendation which led to the planning of Operation Carnival.

One day later Huebner moved into the city himself, taking up his command post in a bunker from where he could control the last offensive operation against the bunker held by Oberst Wilck and his surviving 800 men, who were armed only with light weapons. As the American tank destroyers rumbled towards the ugly concrete bunker, which rose three stories above the ground, with a further two below it, Wilck sent his last message to the headquarters of the Fifteenth German Army. It read 'The Aachen Battle Group is now prepared for the final battle. We have been forced back to a narrow area of ground, but we will defend it to the last man as the Fuehrer wishes.'

But Oberst Wilck did not fight to the last man. The next day the Americans moved up a 155 mm cannon and started pounding the bunker with it at direct range. The great concrete bunker trembled every time one of the huge shells struck it. Down below the lights went out repeatedly and the wounded lying in the long corridors cried out in terror as the plaster from the ceiling fell on their faces. It was too much for Wilck. He ordered two of thirty GIs held prisoner in the bunker to be brought to him and asked if they would risk death to go outside and sur-render the bunker.

The men agreed. While they were gone Wilck shaved and

changed into his last clean uniform. Outside the huge cannon continued its bombardment.

Sometime later the GIs returned with an officer. Wilck discussed terms with him and when they had completed their arrangements, the German Colonel addressed his men for the last time, standing stiff and erect in his clean clothes in front of the shabby, unshaven survivors, some of whom were not quite sober.

'Men', he said, 'it pains me to have to talk to you today. I have been forced to surrender because my supplies of ammunition, food and water are exhausted. I have concluded that any further resistance is foolish. I have acted contrary to my orders which stated I should fight to the last man . . .'

He paused and looked at them sternly. 'I'd like to wish you all the best for your health and a speedy return to our Fatherland when hostilities have ceased so that you can help in the rebuilding of Germany. The American commander tells me I cannot salute you with Sieg Heil or Heil Hitler. But we can do that in our hearts.'

He turned and went out. There was no reaction among the men. Slowly they began to form up into columns to be lead away to the prison camps.

It was mid-day on 21 October, 1944. The Battle for Aachen was over. In the city there remained 1,600 soldiers and 3,500 civilians left alive.

A Czech radio correspondent who was in the city that day gives perhaps the best picture of it at its moment of surrender. Speaking to his radio audience, he reported, 'I have just returned to Brussels after four days of street fighting in Aachen. I have seen the city of German Emperors being wiped out after it had refused the offer of honourable surrender, and I found its people crushed to desperation by a double misery, by our onslaught and by the cruelties of their Nazi masters. We arrived at a huge concrete surface shelter. These shelters are ugly, gloomy constructions with many floors above and below the ground, where hundreds of civilians had been hiding for the last few weeks in darkness and stench. Army officers and the police had the entrance blocked and no one was allowed to leave the place. In the meantime, Gestapo and soldiers were looting the town, grabbing in mad lust the property of their own people, although they had no hope of carrying it away. The Army refused to open the shelter. For several hours, it was besieged by American soldiers, then a German officer offered to surrender, if he was allowed to take away all his things, plus his batman.

'Lt Walker, a young company commander, made no effort to accept such a ridiculous offer and threatened to use flame throwers. That helped. The doors opened and out came the drabbest, filthiest inhabitants of the underworld I have even seen, as people came stumbling out into the light, dazed, then catching a breath of fresh air, and finally starting to jabber, push, scream and curse.

'Some precipitated themselves at me, brandishing their fists. "Where have you been so long," they shouted. "Why didn't you deliver us sooner from those devils." It was a stunning sight. These were the people of the first German town occupied by the Allies. And they were weeping with hysterical joy amidst the smouldering ruins of their homes. "We have been praying every day for you to come," said a woman with a pale, thin face. "You can't imagine what we have had to suffer from them." And then came the insults. Bloodhound, bandit, gangster. All this was levelled at the beloved Fuehrer. There is no one who can hate and curse so thoroughly as the Germans and these people were all full of hate for the Nazis. It was no trick. I certainly would not have been deceived. It was the breakdown of a nation after it had played the wrong cards for five years. Maybe it was the rage of a gangster let down by his gang-leader, but it was a hatred you find only in civil wars.'

The old imperial city was American at last. For the first time in a century a German city had been occupied by a foreign invader. The question was now—what would that foreign invader do with the city?

IV

In the rain that began to fall on Aachen during that third week of October the city presented a scene of sordid horror. Huge piles of brick and stone rubble that had once been proud burghers' houses blocked the streets. Here and there a building still smouldered, its stench joining that of the dead still hidden among the ruins. There was no water, no light, no heat, no sanitation. When the GIs had to pass the open sewers, they held their noses or tied khaki handkerchiefs across their faces. But the victorious men of the 'Big Red One' continued with their task of driving the civilians from the bunkers and cellars in which they had hidden during the siege, and marching them to the big Army barracks at the edge of the city which had been turned into a civilian internment camp.

Here the CIC[1] got down to work investigating the political background of the first sizeable number of German civilians captured since the beginning of World War Two. For the Americans were determined to set up a civilian administration in Aachen under American control and would need reliable people, untainted by Nazism, to run it. The German administration of Aachen was going to be a test case for the rest of the country once the Allied forces had captured it. If the Aachen experiment were successful, its lessons would be applied to the rest of the Reich.

Eagerly the Military Government officials (many of whom had attended crash courses in the management of occupied cities in the United States and Britain, but nevertheless could not speak German), set about finding suitable candidates for the administration among the remaining Aacheners. Most of the higher-ranking officials had fled when the Party had evacuated the city in mid-September, and of those who remained, the Americans rightly guessed that ninety per cent had been party members or intimately connected with the

[1] US Army Intelligence Service.

Nazis. They would not do. Who then should be chosen to run the stricken city?

In the end the American Military Government sought the aid of the Bishop of Aachen. The CIC had already examined the background of the middle-aged Bishop who had chosen to hide in the city rather than escape in September. This and the fact that he had a record of mild resistance to the Nazis convinced the Americans that he would be the right man to turn to for advice about the political background of potential candidates for the new administration. Thus it was that two days after the fall of the city, two American officers, Lt-Col Carmichael, the new town commandant, and his deputy, Major Swoboda, visited the Bishop in his room in the refugee camp at Brand.

For a while the two American officers chatted politely with Bishop van der Velden. Then, through their interpreter, they put the all-important question to the priest. Did he know a trustworthy man capable of taking over the administration of the city? With hardly time for thought, the bishop named the man, who was going to control the destinies of the newly-conquered city for the next six months. 'Oppenhoff—Franz Oppenhoff.'

The American jeep stopped outside the little hunting lodge that Franz Oppenhoff had first rented in September when he had fled from Aachen. At this hideout, situated just outside the Belgian town of Eupen,[1] the former lawyer now spent his time obtaining enough food to feed his pretty young wife and three small children. On that particular afternoon, Oppenhoff was outside the lodge enjoying the sunshine, and when the jeep squealed to a stop he saw, to his great surprise, that next to the American officer, was his old friend the Bishop, sitting very upright and obviously very much out of place.

---

[1] Eupen was German till 1919. Its population was German-speaking and for the first few weeks after its occupation by the Americans the GIs were forbidden to speak to the locals, who were treated as members of an enemy nation.

For once Oppenhoff, with his red hair and freckled face, was at a loss for words. Normally he talked fast and incessantly. Now the sudden appearance of the Bishop in company with an American officer dumbfounded him.

The Bishop, shaking Oppenhoff by the hand, introduced his companions, Major Swoboda and his female interpreter. Swoboda also shook his hand. (Later Oppenhoff was to learn that not all Americans would want to shake the hand of a German.) They went into the little wooden house and Major Swoboda came to the point straight away. 'Oppenhoff,' he asked through his interpreter, 'do you want to help to rebuild the city?'

Franz Oppenhoff looked at the American. He had only a vague idea what the man really meant. 'Rebuild—with what?' But he hesitated only a fraction of a second. Flashing a glance at the Bishop, he said, 'If I said no, our whole life up to now would lose its purpose.' He paused. In that moment, he made a decision that was to cost him his life. 'Yes, I'll help.'

Quickly Major Swoboda brought him up to date, telling him of the catastrophic situation in the conquered city and how its administrative structure had completely collapsed. All that remained was a handful of starving people and a heap of smoking rubble. For the present all Swoboda wanted from Oppenhoff was help to find men who had no Nazi past who could get the city running again. 'They've got to be completely new people— as far as city politics go. Anyone who was an official is no good.' In the crash course on Nazi Germany back in the States, they had taught him that anyone who was a civil servant would automatically be a Nazi. 'No officials, you understand?'

Oppenhoff nodded in acknowledgement. Already his quick mind was running through the friends and acquaintances he had made in his forty years of life in Aachen.

He went to work quickly. Packing a few odds and ends in a battered suitcase, he left his wife and children in Eupen and drove with the Americans to Aachen. He was shocked by what he saw there. Only a few hundred of his fellow citizens were allowed to move about the ruined streets which American bulldozers were now trying to clear of tons of rubble. The rest—nearly six thousand—were spread over four great internment camps, dependent upon the Americans for their meagre rations, save only for what they could find and transport themselves with the help of two tired horses, the only means of transport left in the whole of Aachen.

But Oppenhoff was not easily dismayed. Together with Major Swoboda, he drove from camp to camp, looking for skilled men who were untainted by any association with the Nazis, and who had the specialist knowledge the Americans needed if they were to get the city going again. First of all, he picked his old friend Joseph Hirtz, who, because of his Jewish grandmother, had been suspected by the Nazis. Hirtz, a textile manufacturer, was suggested as Burgomaster for Food, Commerce and Agriculture. Another suggestion was Hans Carl, recommended as the Burgomaster for Labour and Welfare. Carl was a hard-working, fast-talking businessman, who, though not a personal friend of Oppenhoff, seemed to him an ideal choice. Before the war he had run a road transport business between Germany and France and Belgium. He knew how to handle men and he was not prepared to bow obsequiously to the new bosses. As he told an American interrogator, 'I don't give a hang for politics. I am an internationalist, a cosmopolite.' And he added, 'No one wants to work, and I am the most cursed man in town.' Talking of his own class, the relatively wealthy businessmen who had remained in the besieged city, he said, 'Many of them think that because they refused to be evacuated by the Nazis, the Americans should welcome them with open arms.'

Hurrying from camp to camp, Oppenhoff found the men he wanted, some of whom he had known for years, others only for minutes. One of the latter was master-mechanic Walter Bachmann who, up to the fall of Aachen, had owned his own flourishing workshop and now ran the cleaning service of the refugee camp at Brand. One afternoon, a tall man in a grease-stained, grey suit walked up to him while he supervised the cleaning of the camp's latrines. The man raised his hat politely and said, 'Allow me to introduce myself. My name is Oppenhoff. Are you Herr Bachmann?'

The master mechanic nodded.

'Herr Bachmann, I need you. Help me and the other tradesmen too. We've got to get the factories started again . . .'

While Oppenhoff talked on excitedly explaining his purpose in a flood of words, Bachmann, leaning on his broom, stared at him unbelievingly. Did the man really think he could do anything to save Aachen? Besides, who would volunteer for work under these conditions. All that the people in the camp were concerned with was finding enough food to keep alive.

Yet there was something about the man's confidence and urgency that made Bachmann waver. Almost in spite of himself, he found himself saying 'All right, Herr Oppenhoff. I have never had anything to do with local administration. I have no idea of how it works. But something has got to be done. I'll help you.'

One by one, Oppenhoff got his thirty-man team together. But still no decision had been made about who was to be chief burgomaster. And Lt-Col Carmichael, the town commandant, who was concerned about Major Swoboda's tolerance of the Germans, was becoming impatient. On 31 October, he ordered Oppenhoff to have his 30 appointees select the new *Oberbürgermeister* (chief burgomaster) of Aachen by three o'clock that day. He, personally, would swear the new man in in his headquarters, at a ceremony which would be attended by General McSherry and the Supreme Commander's own civilian adviser, Robert Murphy of the State Department.

That morning Swoboda's jeep raced from camp to camp picking up the appointees, who would select the chief burgomaster. Heinrich Faust, an engineer who had worked with Oppenhoff during the war and was to be one of the new burgomasters, was collected from Malmédy in Belgium by a Negro soldier in a jeep. Together they raced along the shell-holed roads to pick up Dr Hans Mies from the camp at Eupen and then on to Raeren to pick up another new burgomaster, Dr Hans Schwipert. With all his passengers aboard, the driver raced down the road towards Aachen, with Faust holding on tightly to two apples, his ration for the day. Mies nudged him and cried, 'If we get out of this alive, I'll be surprised!' He had hardly spoken when the jeep, taking a corner too sharply, careered against the opposite verge and sent its passengers flying in all directions. For a moment, they lay in the mud, dazedly watching the spinning wheels of the upturned jeep. Then, with a groan, the negro got to his feet and started to feel his body carefully. Dr Mies also struggled to his feet and felt his scalp gingerly. A large bump was rapidly rising on the back of his head. Faust looked anxiously for his two apples which had rolled in the mud. Fortunately a group of young American soldiers from a heavy gun emplacement in a nearby field came over and helped to right the vehicle. The driver continued without giving the Germans time to clean off the thick mud which now covered their clothes. The driver knew Colonel Carmichael's temper. It was not safe to be late for an appointment with the Town Commandant of Aachen.

Immediately on arrival in the shattered city the three Germans were led to the former officers' mess of the old Lützow Barracks. It was eleven o'clock. Already some fifteen Germans were assembled there, including Oppenhoff. They sat on the hard wooden chairs facing Major Swoboda, General McSherry and Robert Murphy, with both sides talking softly among themselves. The air was blue with the smoke from the Americans' cigarettes, but not one of the Germans dared to smoke, since they were not supposed to possess US cigarettes and they knew that the *Amis* could not stand their evil-smelling German brands.

When Faust and the other two had taken their seats around the big table, Oppenhoff took the chair and called the meeting to order. Quickly he filled the Germans in on the purpose of todays' assembly and then waited for the question which must come: *Where was Hermann Strater?*

Oppenhoff himself had suggested Hermann Strater, son of an old Aachen family, for the post of chief burgomaster. However, he had learned two days before the election was due to take place that the American CIC had arrested him. Though they had given no reason, presumably they suspected him of being a Nazi. The moment he heard of the arrest, Oppenhoff appealed to Col Carmichael to postpone the election. Carmichael merely replied coldly that it would go ahead as planned and Oppenhoff realized that no amount of arguing would change his mind. Reluctantly he told the others what had happened to Strater. The result was as expected. An angry murmur ran through the assembled group and one mumbled, forgetting the presence of the Americans with their interpreters, 'Well, I think we should not co-operate with them.' It was clear to everyone present whom he meant by 'them'.

Oppenhoff stood up. 'It's no use trying to strike,' he said as calmly as he could. 'If we give up now at this first attempt to co-operate with the Americans, the situation can only deteriorate. Possibly we will be risking the chance of organizing a new city administration by ourselves.'

Oppenhoff's words had their effect. Faust nodded his head energetically, and his mood was soon shared by the others. The tension vanished, replaced by a determination to get on with the job of picking a new chief burgomaster, and in a few minutes the lot had fallen to Oppenhoff himself.

The new mayor realized only too well that the job confronted him with almost insurmountable difficulties; he knew too the dangers of the office. The German line was only a few kilometres away to the east and if the German Army attacked and the *Amis* retreated he could well imagine what his fate would be. He would be strung up on the nearest lamp post. The German radio was making it quite clear in its most recent broadcasts what would happen to 'traitors.'

Oppenhoff warned the newly-elected officials of the risks involved in agreeing to work with the Americans since, in the eyes of their fellows in non-occupied Germany, they were collaborators who deserved nothing better than death. He did not seek to conceal the fact that retribution might be taken against any of their relatives who were living in other parts of Germany, saying 'I am truly concerned for their welfare but my conscience requires me to devote my whole strength to my office in this, the most difficult time in the history of my birthplace.'

A little later the German officials were driven through the wrecked streets to Col Carmichael's offices in the old Suermondt Museum near the cathedral. Oppenhoff was first to enter the building, but he stopped as he opened the door. The place was crowded with reporters in uniform, their pencils and writing pads at the ready. Behind the noisy crowd of allied journalists, the army camera team from the US Signal Corps was setting up their equipment ready to shoot the swearing-in ceremony for the newsreels.

Oppenhoff paled and closed the door behind him again quickly. Major Swoboda turned and said something to the female interpreter. 'What's the matter, Dr Oppenhoff?' she asked.

'The press cameras,' he stuttered. 'Don't you know what that means?'

The girl began to translate what he had said, but Oppenhoff did not give her time to finish. 'If those pictures fall into Nazi hands, I and my family are finished. I would like to request the town commandant to ensure that no names are mentioned and no photographs are taken during the ceremony and, furthermore, I should like to ask Herr Carmichael to ensure that I will not be forced to do anything which will injure the German people or its soldiers.'

When the interpreter had translated, Major Swoboda hurried in through the crowd of curious reporters to Carmichael's room. He knew that Oppenhoff's demands could jeopardize the success of the whole operation. Surprisingly enough, however, Carmichael agreed to let Oppenhoff have his way.

There was a howl of protest from the journalists when he announced that no names and no photos would be allowed, but the Colonel accepted the protest calmly, waiting till every camera had been closed and placed in a position from which no secret snapshots could be taken. Only then did he allow the Germans to enter.

The ceremony was over very quickly. Carmichael indicated through his interpreter that Oppenhoff should raise his right hand and swear an oath of loyalty on the dog-eared Bible in front of him. Rapidly the new Chief Burgomaster repeated the interpreter's words, swearing in the German fashion, raising two fingers instead of the whole hand, but nobody seemed to notice. When it was all over, Oppenhoff, followed by the rest of his new administration, walked through the empty streets.

Soon the correspondents attached to the First US Army were filing their reports, which would flash around the world, 'Hardly ten days after its capture the first German city, Aachen, has formed its own administration from its own citizens.'

Two days later the Allied newspapers bearing the news were flown from the German legation in Spain to Berlin. There, hard-faced men in smart black uniforms duly noted the information and reached for telephones to pass the news on. Both Himmler and the Fuehrer were informed. In the ancient imperial capital a traitor (name unknown) has had the dastardly audacity to allow himself to be appointed chief burgomaster by the enemy. The traitor must be eliminated. *But how and by whom*?

V

Franz Oppenhoff was born in Aachen in 1902. His family had lived in the Rhineland for nearly two centuries, serving the various princelings and bishops of the Rhenish states as lawyers and legal advisers. It was natural then for Franz to become a lawyer and, having graduated from Cologne University, he spent some years working in Berlin before returning to

Aachen to set up his own private practice in January, 1933. It was in that same month that Adolf Hitler accepted the chancellorship of Germany.

Oppenhoff's practice soon began to flourish, helped by the family name and its long association with the law and Aachen. In 1935 he married the daughter of a Rheinish factory owner and before long was the father of three children. At this time Franz Oppenhoff was a typical middle-class Rheinlander, well-to-do and much respected. But a shadow was beginning to cross the life of the happily-married couple. Oppenhoff, a devout Catholic, had as a young man joined the 'Carolingia', the oldest Catholic student organization, and throughout his career, even in far-off Protestant Berlin, he had been interested in the affairs of the Church. Now he found himself having to take sides, as the Nazi régime started putting pressure on certain members of that Church.

The German-Vatican Concordat of 1933, which had been the first official recognition of the Hitler régime by a foreign power, had seemingly regulated the relationship of the Catholic Church to the new Germany, and indeed, the German Church, on a whole, co-operated well enough with Hitler. Yet there were certain exceptions to the rule. The Rhenish priests and the larger cities of the Rhineland, in particular, were not prepared to co-operate with the new masters, not only because of the Nazi's political creed but also because in many Rhinelanders' minds they were associated with the old enemy, Prussia.[1]

When, in 1935, Hitler's troops marched across the Rhine bridges to re-occupy the Rhineland, evacuated by the last Allied troops in 1929, the local brownshirts, aided by the imported Gestapo, went to work to dislodge the clergy, or the Pfaffen[2] as they were contemptuously called. Where it proved impossible to remove a priest quietly to one of the new concentration camps (a British invention during the Boer War, the Nazis would

[1] In fact many of the leading Nazis were non-Prussian. Hitler, for instance, was Austrian, Goebbels a Rhinelander, and Himmler a Bavarian.
[2] A derogatory, German term for a priest.

explain to any curious enquirer), the priest would be forced to appear before a show trial in Cologne or Koblenz. Here, invariably, he would be shown to be sexually corrupt, working for an equally corrupt hierarchy, concerned solely with lining its own pockets with money culled from gullible workers already starving as a result of the world-wide depression.

It was against this background that Franz Oppenhoff found himself faced with an agonizing decision when the Bishop of Aachen asked him to undertake the defence of accused priests. His friends in the legal department warned him off. The new régime would do what it wanted with the priests whether he defended them or not. But Oppenhoff took up the challenge and before long found himself the local champion of the Catholic Church. In 1937 he undertook his first big case of this kind. He accepted the brief to defend a printer named Wilhelm Metz, whose plant had been closed because it had published a papal statement, in spite of the warning by the Gestapo not to do so.

The Metz case proved to be the turning point in his legal career. For two years he fought the state, even though Heydrich himself took a hand in the proceedings and the Gestapo warned Oppenhoff to keep his nose out of the affair. Finally he lost and Metz had his plant taken away, but Oppenhoff's spirited defence of the printer gained him a powerful friend in Johannes Joseph van der Velden, then head of the local seminary, later to become Bishop of Aachen.[1]

Undismayed by his lack of success in the Metz case, Oppenhoff continued to undertake cases which 'no one in his right mind would accept,' as his friends never ceased to warn him. In 1940 when the Wehrmacht overran Belgium, the Gestapo followed, arresting large numbers of officials in the former German cantons of Eupen and Malmédy and accusing them of 'collaboration' with the 'enemy'. Oppenhoff, like many Aacheners, had friends and relatives in the nearby cantons and

[1] From 1943 to 1954.

as a result felt himself duty-bound to accept briefs in defence of the accused.

But time was running out for Oppenhoff. The local Nazi *Kreisleiter*[1] Eduard Schmeer openly called him 'Public Enemy Number One' and the Gestapo searched his offices. At Schmeer's instigation, he started receiving summonses to report for duty with the armed forces: summonses which he only managed to avoid by clever legal artifices. By the summer of 1941 he had had enough. But if he gave up his practice, he would be called up immediately, although he was nearly forty and the father of three young children. In the end a friend came to his rescue and he was offered a management position with the Veltrup Works in Aachen. As the firm was engaged in essential war work he would avoid being called up. So he closed his legal office in the Aachener Wilhelmstrasse, and with his Gestapo file stamped 'National Socialist Reliability Questionable', he went into industry.

For the next three years he kept quiet. He had a good idea what was happening to the opponents of the Nazi régime. He worked hard, concerning himself only with providing enough food for his growing family and with keeping the repeatedly bombed Veltrup Works going. *Kreisleiter* Schmeer still did not leave him in peace, however, and Oppenhoff was regularly confronted with orders to report for military service; but his friends ensured that he did not have to go because he was on 'war essential work'.

In August, 1944, he actually had to report for duty at a small Luftwaffe airfield in the Rhineland some eighty miles away. He was away three days, but when he returned he was still not in uniform, much to the chagrin of Schmeer. But Schmeer now had other things on his mind. Throughout August the Americans barrelled through Belgium and every day saw them that much closer to Aachen. From Cologne the Nazi leader received orders to prepare the frontier city for an active defence.

[1] A local party official.

Oppenhoff could read the writing on the wall too. As the sound of the Allied guns got closer, he realized it was time to leave Aachen. But in which direction should he go? If he moved further inland, it would not be long before he found himself with a rifle in his hand, fighting some desperate rearguard action. What of his family then?

In the end he decided to evacuate himself westwards, taking his family to German-speaking Eupen, from where he could if necessary commute daily to Aachen. It was here that he and his family were surprised in the second week of September, 1944, by the rapidly advancing American tanks.

Since the war Franz Oppenhoff has been celebrated in his home town as a democrat, an ideal to be held up to the rest of the nation for emulation. Yet it is hard to believe that he was what an Anglo-Saxon would understand by 'democrat'. He was more a representative of his class, his religion and his time.

Capt Saul Padover, an American professor of history (who was admittedly prejudiced), interviewed the new Chief Burgomaster just after his appointment. The *sykewar*[1] officer attached to Bradley's 12th Army Group gave this picture of the German. 'On social and economic subjects Oppenhoff was candid to the point of bluntness. I am not sure that he understood the implication of his ideas, or that Americans might view them with distrust as being aggressively anti-democratic, but at any rate he was not a practitioner of the art of concealment. "The whole nation," he said, "can be divided into two categories, those who obey and those who command. Most Germans are afflicted with the sickness of *Kadavergehorsamkeit*,[2] obeying any order like robots, even against their innermost convictions. At the same time these cadaver-obeyers are full of suspicion against each other and hatred for those in authority. This disease, compounded of servile obedience and blind hate, explains Germany's class conflicts and the existence of forty political

---

[1] Psychological warfare.
[2] Literally 'cadaver-obedience'—obeying orders without question.

parties, which, before Hitler destroyed them all, were constantly at each other's throats. I can only hope and pray that the Americans are not going to be foolish enough to permit Germany to have political parties. Heaven help us if parties are allowed to exist. *Dann ist alles aus.* (Then everything is finished.)" '

'As a substitute for political parties, he favoured an authoritarian (but not totalitarian, a distinction without a difference) social structure, not unlike that of Mussolini, Franco, Pétain and such like. He wanted to see the establishment of a labour economy consisting of skilled artisans and divided into masters and apprentices, with the masters in absolute control. Workers were to be placed in fixed categories, without any right to political action or economic demands. No political organization of any kind was to be permitted. No trade unions were to be tolerated. Oppenhoff spoke with impassioned eloquence: "I want to see a small-scale industry organized on paternalistic lines. An employer must have responsibility for his workers, as if they were members of his own family. If we set up such a system we would never have any need for agitations, votings or elections. This is my idea of democracy, true democracy." '

Allowing for distortions due to Captain Padover's own background and political convictions, it is still clear that Franz Oppenhoff was no democrat in the Anglo-American conception of the term. But all the same he was a brave man. Even Padover had to testify to that.

'On one occasion,' Padover wrote, 'he came to me, deeply troubled, and for no reason at all began to lay bare his soul. He said he had risked life and liberty in defending in open court Catholic clergy and part-Jewish businessmen and that his own conscience was, therefore, clear before God. I said, "Herr Oppenhoff, I am no judge of men's souls, nor am I here to pass judgement on any individual." He wanted to know then whether I thought he had no courage because he had avoided serving in the Wehrmacht. I dismissed the thought, but it seemed to obsess him and he said in that husky voice of his, "Believe me, it took more courage to accept this job, to become the First German mayor under American occupation, than to be a soldier at the front. I know that my life is in constant danger. They have threatened to kill me, and I am afraid they will." '

That was the last time that Captain Saul Padover ever saw the Chief Burgomaster. But when he heard of his death, in spite of his admitted prejudices and dislike of Oppenhoff, he wrote, 'I think that Oppenhoff would have been pleased to hear me say what I am saying now—*that he died like a soldier.*'

III

The Werewolves

'New resistance will spring up behind their backs time and time again . . . and like werewolves, brave as death, volunteers will strike the enemy.'

Himmler. November, 1944

On the afternoon of 16 September, 1944, at a routine conference held in his headquarters in East Prussia with Keitel, Goering, Guderian and half-a-dozen other senior officers, Adolf Hitler listened weakly to the daily exposé of the situation on the two major fronts given by the Chief-of-Operations, General Jodl.

Hitler had still not recovered from the shock of the bomb attempt made on him by a group of his officers the previous July. His eyes were dull; gone was that 'hypnotic gaze'; his face was a sickly yellow and there were dark rings under his eyes. While he listened his hands trembled so that at times, he had to press them hard on his lap.

The discussion switched from the east to the west front. Almost casually Jodl mentioned that the hard-pressed German defenders of the western front were getting a bit of a breathing space in the Eifel and Ardennes where over 80 miles of front line were held by only four weak American divisions.

Abruptly at the mention of the Ardennes, Hitler came to life. He stiffened in his chair and raised his flabby hand in a dramatic gesture, 'Stop!' he ordered.

Jodl stopped. The other generals stared attentively at the sick man who a minute before had been slumped so apathetically in his seat. For a moment no one dared breathe. This was the old Hitler. The watery blue eyes and slack mouth had gone. The sick face was suddenly full of life. This was the Hitler who had only known victory.

The Fuehrer leaned forward, 'I am taking the offensive. Here— out of the Ardennes.' He smashed his fist on the unrolled map before him. 'Across the Meuse and on to Antwerp!'

Thus, the idea of the Ardennes Offensive, which Churchill was later to call the 'Battle of the Bulge' was born.

But Germany in the winter of 1944 was not the same country that it had been during the confident summer of 1940 which had brought so many tremendous victories in the west. While the

Wehrmacht still listed ten million men under arms, over four million had been killed since the beginning of the war, with at least 1,200,000 casualties suffered in the last three months alone.

Yet it was not so much the casualties which worried the generals but the general air of defeat that was common to both soldier and civilian. The war had gone on too long, there had been too many air raids and it was clear to even the most fervent Nazi that the defeat of Nazi Germany must be close with two mighty enemy armies—the Russian and the Anglo-American— actually within Germany's borders. Everywhere there were cases of German soldiers surrendering to the enemy with only a token show of resistance so that the Party was forced to order that the family of any soldier who deserted would be arrested and imprisoned; and it was only too obvious from reports culled from the Allied press that many thousands of German civilians were happily co-operating with the enemy in the newly occupied territory. In the early autumn of 1944 while Hitler began to occupy himself almost exclusively with his preparations for the great offensive which would change the whole course of the war, two other Nazi leaders set to work to bolster up the morale of the German Nation—the one through propaganda; the other by active measures to terrorize the faint-hearted.

Josef Goebbels, the German Propaganda Minister, proved himself, above all at this moment, a master of the half-truth and the calculated lie. He was the supreme salesman of the monstrous falsehood that Germany could still win the war if every German devoted himself solely to that end. Well aware of the truth of Hitler's statement in *Mein Kampf* that, 'The art of propaganda consists precisely in being able to awaken the imagination of the public through an appeal to their feelings,' Goebbels seized upon the American Morgenthau Plan[1] with glee.

[1] The Plan, named after its originator Henry J. Morgenthau, envisaged, in essence, that a conquered Germany should be converted into a 'country primarily agricultural and pastoral in character'.

When details of the plan appeared in the American press in September, 1944, Goebbels quickly made use of them to illustrate to the German people the dire consequences of defeat. Already he had instilled a deep fear of the Russians into the Germans and now he set about trying to convince them, with the aid of the Plan, that the British and Americans were no better. 'The Jew Morgenthau,' his Berlin Radio announced that month, 'sings the same tune as the Jews in the Kremlin.' His *Völkischer Beobachter*, the chief Nazi newspaper, stated that the plan would mean 'the destruction of German industry to such an extent that fifty per cent of the German population would be faced with starvation or would be forced to emigrate as working slaves . . . Germany has no illusions about what is in store for her people if they do not fight with all available means against an outcome that would make such plans possible.'

His words and deeds began to have an effect. The output of the war factories started to rise again in spite of the Allied bombing. 'Total mobilization,' as Goebbels named his drive to supply the Army with more manpower became the order of the day. In September he was able to produce 200,000 recruits for Hitler's new offensive and in October a further 200,000. In 1943, when it had first seemed possible that Germany might lose the war, Goebbels had cried out to an audience of workers and soldiers, '*Wollt Ihr den totalen Krieg?*'[1] and had received a tremendous burst of spontaneous applause as an answer. Now at last Goebbels was giving the German Nation its 'total war'.

But there was another Nazi leader who involved himself in the bolstering-up of the German will to fight—Heinrich Himmler, head of the SS and Commander-in-Chief of the Home Army.[2] The most feared man in Europe was essentially a desk worker with a pedantic head for details. He had no real

[1] Do you want total war?
[2] He was in charge of all reserve, training and recruiting formations in Germany itself.

capacity for leadership, but he did have the means to 'coerce and punish those who failed or refused to be organized'.

That autumn his chief task was to replace the divisions lost during the summer battles in west and east. In August he set about raising and training twenty-five *Volksgrenadier* divisions.[1] In August, 1944, addressing a group of Gauleiters in Posen, he told them, 'In my order of the day I gave this new army the name of the National Socialist People's Army. I asked the Fuehrer—and he agreed—that the new divisions should be given the name of People's Grenadier Divisions. I rejected the idea of the *Reichswehr*[2] and everything to do with it. I had to find a name. I believe at this moment we are waging a people's holy war; I believe that the army which must win this war, and with which we shall win it, is the National Socialist People's Army; the name indicates unequivocally that this army must be indelibly stamped with the doctrine of National Socialism.'

Hand in hand with these measures undertaken by *der treue Heinrich* (the loyal Heinrich) as the Fuehrer had once called him, Goebbels' *Völkischer Beobachter* conducted its psychological indoctrination campaign in a rising crescendo. Everything was pressed into service for the cause of the 'people's holy war'—the new *Volksgrenadier* divisions, the terrifying secret weapons soon to be launched on the allies, ceaseless propaganda about the fate in store for Germany under the Morgenthau Plan. The climax was reached on 19 October when the paper's red banner headline announced that 'To Commemorate The Battle of Nations[3] the Fuehrer Announces the Formation of the *Volkssturm*!'

In effect the *Volkssturm* was a *levee en masse*, a local militia, somewhat resembling the Home Guard, comprising all men 'capable of bearing arms in defence of the Fatherland' between

[1] People's Grenadier Divisions, somewhat smaller in size than the old Wehrmacht divisions, but better armed with automatic weapons.

[2] The pre-1933 name of the German Army.

[3] Fought at Leipzig against Napoleon in 1813. Called the 'Battle of Nations' because of the many nations involved on the side opposing Napoleon.

the ages of 16 and 60. Although politically and administratively it was nominally under the control of Hitler's 'Grey Eminence' Martin Bormann, it was militarily under the command of Himmler, who later, when it went into action, refused to give any other departments information about his pet project.

Three days before the fall of Aachen, Himmler inspected the first unit of the newly established *Volkssturm*. After he had walked up and down the ranks filled with old men in civilian clothes, armed with Czech rifles and fanatical Hitler Youths in their black uniforms with their Panzerfausts tilted confidently over their narrow young shoulders, he took the opportunity presented by the anniversary of the victory over Napoleon to make a speech. Quoting the situation in Prussia at that time and the weapons possessed by the *Landsturm*, the Prussian *levee en masse* of 1813, 'All kinds of fowling pieces with and without bayonets, spits, cudgels, hayforks, sabres and straightened scythes,' he went on to warn the Allies what they could expect now they had crossed Germany's frontiers, ending with the words which Allied intelligence officers duly noted: 'In the territory too, where they believe they have conquered us, new resistance will spring up behind their backs time and time again . . . *and like werewolves, brave as death, volunteers will strike the enemy!*'

For the first time the organization which was not yet formed but which later would cause so much fear and uncertainty in Allied ranks, had been mentioned in public. *The Werewolves!*

II

Himmler had been personally offended by the fall of Aachen. He had been in the city just before the siege had begun and had promised his audience of party leaders that Aachen would never be evacuated. Though he was a man rarely given to anger, the whole sorry role played by the local party bosses in the siege had infuriated him. Schmeer, the *Kreisleiter* of Aachen, was dismissed from his party office, flung out of the Party itself and sent to the front as a common soldier, primarily because of the way he had bungled the evacuation of the civilian population. Now Himmler's assistants were reporting to him that several thousand civilians who had remained in Aachen had welcomed the Americans as if they were liberators, and that the enemy press was full of their anti-Nazi statements to eager reporters, interviewing their first German civilians.

In a letter to the SS Police Chief for the West[1] General Karl Gutenberger, he wrote angrily: 'From the enemy press it is clear that in some areas occupied by the Anglo-Americans the local population is behaving in a manner without honour. I order that immediately these areas have been recaptured, the guilty parties should be brought to justice. Now we should attempt to 'educate' the population in question by the execution of the death penalty *behind the front*' (my italics).

The task of carrying out such executions was given to the Werewolf Organization formed in November, 1944, as *Unternehmen Werwolf* (Enterprise Werewolf). Under Himmler's authority the new secret authority was to be responsible for guerrilla warfare behind the Allied lines. It was to be a paramilitary organization, trained by the Waffen SS (Armed SS), to fight behind the front as a diversionary force and thus assist the regular German Army. In other words, it was never intended to operate independently of the High Command and indeed most of the young men and women who were later to join the organization never realized that they might be expected to wear civilian clothes during their operations instead of uniforms. The discovery that they would go into action in mufti and thus risk the danger of being shot on capture, occasioned many of them to desert as soon as they had an opportunity to do so.

That November Himmler gave the command of the new highly secret organization (which he, for security purposes, always referred to as 'W') to SS Police General Pruetzmann, a member of his staff.

[1] The Rhineland.

1. *Jost Saive and Mlle Straat. This photo-graph was taken shortly before Saive's death.*

2. *Erich Morgenschweiss, aged 16.*

3. *The monument marks the spot where Jost Saive was killed.*

4. *General Huebner, CO of 1st Division, the 'Big Red One' which captured Aachen.*

5. *A US Engineer using a mine-detector outside the Hotel Quellenhoff, lately the HQ of the German Army.*

6. *US troops entering Aachen.*

Pruetzmann had long been a member of the Party and the SS. In July, 1941, he had been sent to Russia by the Fuehrer as one of the Party's principal representatives, who, together with the notorious Erich von den Bach-Zelewski and Ober-gruppenfuehrer Friedrich Jeckeln, was responsible for police security in the newly occupied territories. It had been Hans Pruetzmann's task, with the aid of a regiment of police, certain SS units and local 'volunteers', to introduce the 'New Order' to these territories, by terrorizing the local population.

The actual number of Jews and other 'Unreliable elements' murdered by Pruetzmann's unit cannot now be established, but it is known that the three SS units put to death some 200,000 Jews by the time operations were suspended at the end of 1941.

In the year that followed Pruetzmann was given the task of 'exporting' children from the Baltic states for 'Germanization' and when he had completed this he was posted to the Ukraine where he came into conflict with Gauleiter Koch, who had charge of a huge Russian province. Koch felt Pruetzmann was spying on him and missed no opportunity of snubbing the SS General. Soon he forbade Pruetzmann to accept Himmler's orders and the two men began to fight quite openly.

In the end the Red Army ended the feud between the Gauleiter and the SS General by recapturing the Ukraine. Pruetzmann returned to the Reich, where he was given a post on Himmler's staff. There he gained the reputation of being vain and idle, running his office so inefficiently that Schellenberg, a fellow SS General, remonstrated with Himmler to close it down.

Schellenberg's remonstrances had some effect, for Himmler decided that, rather than give command of the Werewolf Organization to Pruetzmann, he would put in charge a man whom the Americans were soon to dub 'the most wanted man in Europe', SS Colonel Otto Skorzeny.

Skorzeny was already a legend in Germany. After joining the *Leibstandarte*[1] in 1940 as a private he had quickly risen through the ranks until in 1941 he had been wounded and

[1] The First SS Division—'Adolf Hitler's Bodyguard'.

returned to Berlin, passed fit only for limited duty. But he was not the kind of man to be tied to a desk job for long and by the end of that year he found himself in charge of the new secret German commando force, which had been inspired by the success of the British organization. Skorzeny flung himself into the new task with tremendous energy, recruiting not only Germans but volunteers from half-a-dozen other European nations for the highly dangerous work.[1] Soon he had built an élite force of intelligent, fearless young men who were skilled linguists as well as experienced soldiers and parachutists. In 1943 Skorzeny brought off his first and perhaps greatest coup when, with a force just short of a hundred men, he engineered the rescue of the Italian dictator Benito Mussolini, who had been imprisoned in the Gran Sasso, a supposedly impregnable mountain position, by the new Italian Government. The operation carried out by means of glider troops brought Otto Skorzeny the Knight's Order of the Iron Cross from Hitler and gained him the reputation of being a man able to undertake the toughest and most hair-raising kinds of operation with success.

In late November Himmler summoned Skorzeny to his new headquarters near the village of Hohenlychen. The Reichs-führer introduced Skorzeny to the other men present, Schellenberg, Kaltenbrunner and Pruetzmann. Then he got down to business. He explained that the purpose of the discussion was to ensure that the new Werewolf was properly organized. Up to now it had been left to individual Gauleiters and SS police chiefs to set up the new resistance movement, each in his own individual way. But, according to Himmler, their efforts were not good enough. The Organization needed a firm, efficient hand. Pruetzmann looked down at his papers as Himmler said to Skorzeny, 'I think that this would really

[1] As most of the equipment he needed for his work could not be obtained in Germany at that time, Skorzeny, using double agents in Holland, convinced the various exile governments in England to drop the required equipment for the 'resistance'. The 'resistance' was Skorzeny.

be your kind of work, . . . Or do you have enough on your plate already?'[1] Skorzeny thought quickly. During the course of the German retreat eastwards after the Allied invasion of Normandy, he had built up a network of agents in France and Belgium, but so far he had had little success with his organization. Had he now time, in the light of what Hitler expected him to do in the Ardennes, to build up a third organization? He decided he had not.

'Herr Reichsfuhrer,' he said, 'I feel I have enough to do already.'

Himmler thought for a moment, then turning to Pruetzmann, he said to the others, 'May I introduce you to the new head and organizer of the Werewolf?'

Quickly the group started to discuss details and it was agreed that Skorzeny would place the resources of his Berlin depot at the disposal of the new organization. Pruetzmann would be allowed to draw special weapons as well as captured Allied equipment and clothing from it (although Skorzeny already knew he did not have the supplies to clothe his own special 'jeep teams' for the Ardennes operation).

Then the subject of the Werewolf was dropped and Himmler, who never lacked the ability to lose himself completely in the wildest of projects, began to pick Skorzeny's brains on the current state of the new 'vengeance weapons'—the V1's and V2's. 'Do you mean,' he asked Skorzeny 'that one could bombard New York with a V1?'

'Yes,' Skorzeny assured him, 'using a U-boat as the firing point.' Himmler concluded the conversation enthusiastically, saying he would immediately inform the Fuehrer and Admiral Doenitz that it would soon be possible to bombard New York by means of these new V1's.

---

[1] Presumably Himmler knew that Skorzeny had already been assigned the job (by Hitler himself) of organizing top secret sabotage teams, dressed in U.S. uniforms and speaking fluent English, who were to penetrate behind the US lines in the first days of the planned Ardennes offensive to cause as much disruption as they could (which they did in a spectacular manner).

Skorzeny left at this point, glad to be free of the responsibility of having to take over an organization whose only original feature was its name. Let Pruetzmann see how he could manage with that particular headache.

But if Pruetzmann was lazy and inefficient, he did know he was already stamped as a war criminal, who would be brought to justice if the Allies won the war. It was all too clear to him that, should this happen, he would certainly be executed.

Accordingly he did his best to carry out the top secret order to form the Werewolf.

In the main he saw two areas where his Werewolves could be successfully employed—in that part of East Prussia already captured by the Russians, where there were still large numbers of Germans who had not fled before the advancing Red Army, who could help to hide and feed the guerrillas; and in the Eifel area in the west between Aachen and Prüm where, in addition to German inhabitants who might help, the new German offensive was soon to be launched.

It was to the Gauleiters of the districts bordering on these two areas that he sent his first messages requesting them to find suitable men and women—and boys and girls—who would volunteer to take part in clandestine operations behind enemy lines in the near future. Soon the names of the first volunteers—'P-men' or 'Pruetzmen' as they were called in the first days as a cover—began to flood into his Berlin office. By the end of the year there were some 4,000 to 5,000 of them, eager, fanatical young men and women, drawn mainly from the Nazi youth organizations, the Waffen SS, and special sabotage units. The wolves had begun to join the pack.

The man responsible for recruiting, training and organizing the Werewolf in the West was SS Police General Gutenberger, who had been a member of the Party since 1925. Once the Nazis came to power he made a rapid career in the Party, advancing to police chief of the Ruhr industrial city of Duisburg. Four years later as SS Police General he took over command of the whole western area of Germany.

It was Gutenberger's job to supervise the political activities of both the civilians and servicemen under his command. Every day he sent confidential reports to Berlin, passing on the weaknesses and slips of even the highest ranking officers. 'Col Feind, Düren—lax in his attitude to duty and should be dismissed . . . Lt-Col Buhrmann, Krefeld 60J—unwilling to take responsibility, no power of decision. Dismissal urgently necessary . . . Col Kaehler, Neuss—politically colourless, no power of decision, dismissal necessary.' It was an easy life far from the front. A telephone call and a man could lose his job. One signature and men and women could be hauled off to prison. A word in the right direction and the 'guilty party' could disappear for ever.

It was, therefore, with no particular pleasure that Karl Gutenberger learned in the first week of November, 1944, that he was going to receive a visit from Himmler's 'special representative', General Pruetzmann. He knew Hans Pruetzmann of old and had long come to the conclusion that wherever Pruetzmann made his appearance it meant trouble and extra work. Gutenberger was not mistaken.

Pruetzmann appeared in his usual black Horch, followed by another large limousine filled with the members of his bodyguard, tall, healthy young men, whom Gutenberger thought would have served their country better at the front than watching over Pruetzmann. But the chief of the new organization gave Gutenberger little time to dwell on the defects of his personality. After a short conference in which he explained the role of *Unternehmen Werwolf*, he asked Gutenberger to accompany him to the Gauleiters of Cologne and Düsseldorf. As old party men they would know the right local people he would need to build up his secret organization in the west.

Reluctantly Gutenberger drove with the Pruetzmann cavalcade to Cologne and then on to Düsseldorf. There Pruetzmann left him to drive on to Essen where he was to confer alone with the Gauleiter of that city. But before Pruetzmann set

off, he turned to Gutenberger and said, 'Incidentally, Gutenberger, what have you done about Aachen?'

Gutenberger looked at him in bewilderment for a moment.
'Aachen?'

'Yes that swine whom the *Amis* have made chief burgomaster.'

'What about him?' Gutenberger asked, but he knew what
Pruetzmann was going to say before he said it.

'*Dan mussen Sie doch umlegen, nicht wahr.*'[1]

'Yes,' Gutenberger said, 'I know'. But he said the words
without conviction.

For the first time mention had been made of the intention to
murder Franz Oppenhoff.

III

In the next weeks Gutenberger went quickly ahead with the
training of the volunteers for 'P-men', which the Gauleiters of
Cologne, Düsseldorf and Essen sent him. These recruits were
drawn mainly from the Hitler Youth or the Union of German
Maidens, who had known nothing else but the Nazi creed
for most of their young lives. All of them had held some full-
time position in the Party youth organizations and as a result
both the boys and girls could use most of the small arms
weapons used by the German Army, be it revolver, machine
pistol or bazooka. What they did not know was how to use
explosives and how to behave in enemy-occupied territory,
though, because of the way they had been recruited, virtually
all of them were intimately acquainted with the border area in
which they would eventually operate.

It was Gutenberger's job to ensure that they received training
in these two activities and he delegated this task to two men.
One was SS Col Raddatz, a former school master who, at the
beginning of the war, had volunteered as a private for the
Leibstandarte. Here he rose to the rank of captain and after

---

[1] Roughly—'You've got to bump him off, you know'.

being wounded at the battle for Caen just after the Allied Invasion he had been posted to Gutenberger's staff. The other, Lt-Col Neinhaus, was an old party friend of Gutenberger, who, as a former regular officer with service in World War One, had been employed in recruiting in Cologne until he had an argument with the local SS recruiters. As a result he had requested a transfer, but before that transfer had come through he had met Gutenberger by chance while the latter was visiting the Gauleiter of Cologne with Pruetzmann. Recognizing his old acquaintance, Gutenberger had asked him if he would like to come to his headquarters 'on a special assignment'. Knowing that anyone who had fallen foul of the Waffen SS could expect trouble, Neinhaus had readily agreed. Now he found himself under Raddatz's somewhat pedantic command, trying to build up this new and very mysterious organization.

The two colonels picked Schloss Hülchrath as the ideal location for their training activities, since it was soon to be vacated by part of Gutenberger's staff, and could readily be placed at their disposal. Schloss Hülchrath was set in the middle of a small medieval village of the same name not far from the Rhenish town of Erkelenz. Two main roads passed to north and south of it connecting the village with the Ruhr as well as to the territories already occupied by the enemy. Yet no main road ran through the village itself. Thus, Hülchrath was well situated for speedy movement west or east, but it was not open to prying eyes.

Similarly the castle itself, which dated back to the fourteenth century, was ideally suited for the training of an underground organization. Surrounded by a circle of medieval half-timbered houses inhabited by the villagers, which shielded it from the cobbled village street, it could only be entered by a narrow gateway which was easily guarded. There was, as an added safeguard, another inner keep, separated from the outer circle of houses by a large bare courtyard; this keep too could only be entered by one narrow gate. It was in the inner keep that Colonel Neinhaus set up his training headquarters.

While the first batch of fifty volunteers, who included some miners from the Ruhr, as well as Hitler Youth, settled into their new quarters and were fitted out with SS uniforms so that their cover story of being members of the *Wachkompanie der Waffen SS*[1] looked genuine to the locals, Neinhaus set out to tour the front between Kleve and Schmidthein.

This was the area held by the German Army Group B, commanded by Field Marshal Model, whose intelligence officers now assisted Neinhaus in finding sites for the bunkers his people would use later. Colonel Neinhaus' plan was that the Werewolves should allow themselves to be *überrollt*—'over-run'—by the Advancing Allied troops. They would then take refuge in the underground bunkers, most of which were dug into the hillsides of the rugged Eifel mountains, and were well stocked with food and arms, from whence they would sally forth at night to attack the enemy in the rear. During the day-time they could wander through the Allied-held villages dressed in civilian clothes and armed with forged papers provided by the Gestapo security man and spy-catcher Stubenrauch who was also attached to his staff.

Meanwhile back in the castle, the volunteers set about their training exercises, carrying out their theoretical training in closely-guarded second floor rooms in the keep during the daytime and sallying out late at night to practice the new techniques they had learnt under cover of darkness.

For over a month Karl Gutenberger heard no more from Pruetzmann. Although the Allied advance had bogged down in the bitter fighting of the Hurtgen Forest, he knew that it would not be long before they started to push forward again, an eventuality for which he had to be prepared. Meanwhile he was in daily contact with Raddatz, who kept his superior informed of what progress the 'P-Men' were making at Schloss Hülchrath, taking up far too much of Gutenberger's precious time with his long-winded reports. In his own mind, the SS Police General had quietly decided to drop the murder plan.

[1] Guard Company of the Armed SS.

Every morning when he woke he could hear the Allied guns roaring in the Eifel. One day not too far off those guns would be on the Rhine and Germany would be finished. What then? He was realist enough to know that, as a high ranking SS officer, he would automatically be sent to prison. But if the *Amis* sent him to jail they would have to free him one day. There was, however, no hope even of this if he were responsible for a murder, even though that murder could be interpreted as a legitimate act of war.

Karl Gutenberger was a family man and was determined that come what may he would survive the war. The murder of the chief burgomaster of Aachen because of some stupid whim of Pruetzmann's was certainly not part of his plans for the future. He was not going to risk his neck just for that.

In the first week of December Gutenberger received a shock. One of his aides brought a top secret telex message from Himmler himself. After ordering that 'every burgomaster in the territory occupied by the Americans is to be shot,' Himmler asked the question which Gutenberger had dreaded would come sooner or later, 'What has been done in the matter of the chief-burgomaster of Aachen?'[1]

With a sinking feeling Karl Gutenberger knew there was no way out; he would have to go ahead with the murder plan after all.

IV

At 0530 hours precisely on the morning of 16 December, 1944, two thousand German guns crashed into action along the

[1] Gutenberger excused his lack of action by telling Himmler over the telephone that he had 'personnel difficulties and so it was not possible to get through enemy lines.' Presumably Himmler did not believe his subordinate, but although the two SS leaders did not like each other, he let Gutenberger get away with it for a little longer.

eighty-five miles of Ardennes front between Monschau in Germany, in the north, and Echternach in Luxemburg, in the south. Up in the snowy, fog-cloaked heights of the German Schneifel, hundreds of tanks concealed in the fir forests began to rumble out of their hiding places to support the white-clad infantry. One minute later a railway gun in the German town of Prüm started lobbing huge 14 inch shells at the little Belgian road and rail centre of St Vith, the first key town which had to be taken. The Ardennes Offensive, 'Hitler's last gamble', was underway.

With some 250,000 men divided into three armies, two tank and one infantry, Hitler hoped to advance to the River Meuse and cross it south of Liege on the fourth day of the attack. From there his tank columns would race for Antwerp, the Allies' chief supply port on the Continent. Once this had been captured, Hitler would have cut off the major portion of Allied supplies and at the same time divided the British and American armies. As a result he hoped that he could put off the end of the war for a few more months and thus gain more favourable terms for Germany than those of the official Allied policy of 'unconditional surrender'. In addition, he felt that if the war continued for a few more months there would be a clash between the Western Allies and Russia, probably over the Balkans, where already the British and the Russians were in conflict, with a resultant breakdown of the Alliance which could only be to Germany's advantage.

Gutenberger, while doubting in the efficacy of the counter-attack which was for the moment throwing back the Allied forces, welcomed it because it gave him an opportunity to postpone the unpleasant assignment with which Pruetzmann had landed him. He secretly hoped that the murder of the chief burgomaster of Aachen would be forgotten altogether in the course of the offensive. Accompanied by his staff he drove from Germany to a small village near St Vith, where he set up his headquarters to await its fall. Once it and the other border towns and villages had been recaptured, it would be his task as

SS Police Chief to 'clean them up'—the euphemistic phrase to describe the imprisonment and worse of 'unreliable elements'.

The surprise German counter-offensive threw the remaining civilian inhabitants of Aachen into a panic. The German line was only a few miles away from the Allied-held city and the civilians were used to gunfire; but the barrage of the morning of 16 December was different.

When it was followed a little while later by the explosion of the first V1's (whether these 'revenge weapons', as the Germans called them, were intended for the Belgian city of Liege and had fallen short or whether they had been aimed deliberately at the German city under American occupation, no one was ever able to find out) and they saw American trucks bringing in grim-faced infantry to help stem the counter-offensive, the few thousand Germans who remained in the city realized that their fellowcountrymen were attacking in earnest.

In the offices occupied by the Americans employed in the Military Government, it was clear that the officers and enlisted men were no less disturbed than the Germans. They sat at their desks with their helmets on and their carbines across their desks, while outside the engines of their jeeps were warmed up every fifteen minutes. In the coldest winter that Western Europe had experienced in the last thirty years no one wanted to fall into enemy hands because his vehicle wouldn't start.

For a while Oppenhoff, who thanked God in his prayers every day that he had left his wife and children back in Belgian Eupen, managed to calm the panic that broke out among his administration. 'God and the High Venn[1] will protect us,' he told his alarmed colleagues as the sound of gunfire daily grew louder.

One day the rumour spread through the town that the SS had already set up the gallows for them at the town of Euskirchen some twelve miles away. 'Thank God for the gallows,' Dr Mies broke the silence of the assembled administrators when

[1] A high mountain ridge a little south of Aachen.

they heard the rumour. 'I don't feel like being chief actor in one of Goebbels' show trials staged on the steps of the town hall!'

Then Josef Hirtz, a half-Jewish clothing manufacturer, dispelled any remaining tension when he quipped, 'You don't need to worry, Mies, with your two metre figure.[1] While you're standing on the tips of your toes and looking down at the people present, we'll be already hanging.'

But in reality, there was nothing to joke about. Even the Allied-controlled *Aachener Nachrichten*, the first newspaper authorized by the Allies in Germany, could not hide the seriousness of the situation in the Ardennes; and at night anyone who cared to break the curfew and glance out of his blacked-out door could spot the angry red stabs of the German artillery everywhere in the surrounding hills.

In the end Franz Oppenhoff headed a delegation to Lt-Col Carmichael. Dispensing with ·the aid of an interpreter for security reasons, Oppenhoff and his colleagues forcefully demanded that Carmichael protect them if the Americans were driven from Aachen.

The American Colonel listened to their demands in silence. Then he told them to wait and disappeared into an inner room to telephone his superiors. Because of the German offensive, priorities for the military telephone net were very high and it was ten minutes before he returned and promised them that if the city had to be evacuated, they would be taken back by the American garrison. They heaved a collective sigh of relief.

But Franz Oppenhoff had other problems than the threat posed by the Ardennes Offensive. It was becoming increasingly clear to him that the Americans were very difficult people to deal with. For the smallest thing he had to wait for hours in Carmichael's or Swoboda's office, invariably only to be told 'I'll see what I can do for you,' a phrase he had come to know by heart, although he spoke hardly a word of English. Usually this meant that nothing was done.

[1] Dr Mies was the largest of the men present, being some 1·89 metres, about 6 ft 3 inches.

In Paris General Eisenhower decreed that there would be no fraternization between the Germans and their conquerors. Allied soldiers would only address German civilians when their military duties demanded it, nothing more. When the order reached Major Swoboda, who up to this time had been friendly towards the Chief Burgomaster, he ordered Oppenhoff to come to his office at once. Swoboda received him coldly without his usual exchange of greetings. Oppenhoff noted too that the American refused to take his out-stretched hand. The Major turned to Liesel Greven, who had spent several years in England and now acted as Oppenhoff's interpreter, and said, 'It is very important that you translate my words exactly.' Then looking directly at Oppenhoff, he continued, 'I have some unpleasant news for you. General Eisenhower has ordered a non-fraternization rule. From now onwards all personal contact with Germans is forbidden. Every conversation with them is to be limited to the very minimum. Thank you. That is all.'

Oppenhoff stood looking at the American in disbelief. He had known the Major for two months now. They had celebrated Christmas together. Indeed it was only due to his presence that he had been able to invite more than three of his colleagues for a drink at Christmas, since the Americans had strict regulations about the assembly of more than three German civilians. But Major Swoboda merely stared back at him in silence. Oppenhoff turned and went out.

Now the Americans, shocked and angered by what they regarded as the 'European Pearl Harbor',[1] displayed a sudden brutality in their dealings with German civilians. When the infantry, fighting in the snows of the Ardennes, needed sheets to camouflage themselves, a requisition order went out and GIs swarmed through the few houses still occupied by the local population, not only seizing bed-sheets and white tablecloths, but throwing whole beds through the windows into the street below. After watching this senseless destruction of furniture and

[1] The Ardennes Counter-attack.

household goods already in short supply, Oppenhoff went to Lt-Col Carmichael to protest. He did not find Carmichael but another American officer told him, 'You can be happy that our soldiers work off their anger with furniture. You Germans do it with human beings.'

And if the *Amis* weren't bad enough, his own fellow-countrymen started to cause trouble. A wave of denunciation broke out under the stress caused by the Offensive. The CIC began to arrest completely innocent Aacheners who had been denounced by their neighbours as 'Nazis and spies'.

As the Ardennes Offensive reached its crescendo, Oppenhoff grew steadily more despondent. Living in the most primitive conditions without his wife and children to cheer him up, he sat at night in his candle-lit room which was completely without heat, nursing a single glass of schnapps and brooding over his situation. Time and again he told his fellow councillors, 'It's no use. No one wants to help us!' And his colleagues would watch him with serious faces. They knew that if Oppenhoff gave up, the whole city administration would collapse completely—and the Americans would never be able to resurrect it in a city which was divided into a score of warring factions, each out to gain the most advantage for itself.

But in the morning Franz Oppenhoff would have shaken himself out of his depression and be at his desk in his tiny dark office.

V

Ilse Hirsch felt that the Ardennes Offensive was almost a personal reward for all the hard work she had done in the last few weeks since the German patrol had rescued her from the hunting lodge near Monschau. All the help she had given in building bunkers and defensive lines in the Eifel had been worthwhile after all, for it was in these bunkers that the Sixth SS Panzer Army, now fighting deep inside Belgium, had hidden its equipment and men. For the moment she rested in Cologne, her time divided between her dull routine duties in the office of the local Hitler Maiden Headquarters and those few exhilarating moments standing expectantly around the *Volksempfänger*[1] listening to the harsh dramatic blare of the brass trumpets and roll of drums which heralded another *Siegesmeldung*[2] in the Ardennes. But the routine existence in Cologne was not to last for long. In the last week of December she was summoned to see Hilde Schulze, head of the local Hitler Maiden organization, who knew of Ilse's adventure at Monschau.

The head of the Hitler Maidens came to the point immediately. 'You were in Monschau from February, 1942, to April—or May—1944?'

'April, 1944, *Gebietsmädelfuhrerin*.'[3] Ilse corrected her in the approved military fashion.

'And from then on you were in Aachen till it was evacuated?'

'Yes.'

'Good,' the woman made a note on the paper in front of her on the desk. 'So you know that part of the Eifel well?' She looked up and stared hard at Ilse Hirsch. Then she bent down to her papers again and with a wave of her hand, she dismissed her.

Two days later Ilse Hirsch found herself posted to Düsseldorf-Lohausen, where she was ordered to report to *Standartenfuehrer* Raddatz. The SS man received her kindly enough. He asked her to sit down and offered her a cigarette which she hastily declined. '*Eine deutsche Frau schminkt sich nicht und eine deutsche Frau raucht nicht*.'[4] Those were the two lessons she had tried to drum into her teenage female charges for years now.

---

[1] People's Receiver, the standard German wireless set during this period.

[2] Victory Proclamation.

[3] Area Organizer.

[4] A German woman does not use make-up and a German woman does not smoke.

For a few moments the SS officer, who, she could tell from his speech, was an *Akademiker*, a graduate, chatted idly about the war and her job, then he asked her how well she knew the Aachen area. She told him of her years in the area, during the war and before it when she had worked as an apprentice in Umbreit's Bookshop a dozen or so miles from Aachen.

The SS officer nodded thoughtfully, and said, 'We need women for our operations. You know, men cannot go out after curfew, but they wouldn't worry too much about a lone *harmless* woman on the streets after hours.' He lingered a little over the word 'harmless', a slight amused smile decorating his lips. She wondered what curfew he meant and who 'they' were. But six years in the Party had taught her not to ask questions and she remained silent. 'So Fraulein Hirsch,' the SS man continued, 'I think we can find a use for you. I shall send you from here to Schloss Hülchrath, near Erkelenz. Lt Wenzel will meet you there. He'll put you in the picture about "Operation Carnival".'[1]

Ilse Hirsch had been born in the Ruhr Industrial town of Hamm in 1922. Her father, a master tailor, lost his first wife, Ilse's mother, when she was five. A short time later the master tailor married again and Ilse was packed off to a boarding school.

Ilse remained at her convent until she passed her secondary leaving certificate. She then did another year in a private college, again run by the Ursuline Nuns, finally leaving to become a kindergarten nurse. She soon gave this up to enter the service of what is called in Germany a *Kunstgewerblerin*.[2] Here in the little apartment behind the Umbreit's shop in Euskirchen, Ilse Hirsch found a home for the first time since her step-mother had sent her away to boarding school seven years before.

---

[1] There is some confusion about what was said at this interview. Later Ilse Hirsch stated that Raddatz said her task was to help murder the burgomaster of Aachen and that the murder team 'would fly to Aachen'. Raddatz denied this and for once might have been telling the truth; at that time it had not yet been decided that Operation Carnival would be launched by air.

[2] A dabbler in art.

7. *Schloss Hülchrath, the secret training centre of the Rhineland Werewolves.*

8. *British paratroopers examining a dead Werewolf, shot as he sniped at British troops near Lübeck, 3/4 May, 1945.*

9. *The spot where Chief Burgomaster Oppenhoff was murdered on Palm Sunday, 1945.*

At the age of sixteen she had already joined the Union of German Maidens as a form of protest against the nuns who wanted piety not politics. Now in her spare time, she started to instruct the younger members of that organization in handiwork, modelling and similar skills. They met in the evenings, working around a long table, their needles clicking busily as they knitted sweaters for the soldiers on the eastern front, listening intently to Ilse or some other enthusiastic *Führerin* reiterate the Fuehrer's life history, which by now everyone knew backwards. 'Born in Austria in 1889, Adolf Hitler soon showed that talent for leadership when at the age of sixteen, he . . .'

In latter years Ilse Hirsch often denied that she had ever subscribed to the cult of Hitler worship; yet for the love-starved adolescent girl who had never known any real affection at home, the community of the Nazi youth organization assumed an immense importance. For the first time in her life she belonged to something.

In 1941 her industry, dedication and 'artistic' talents came to the attention of the older women who ran the organization. She was asked to take over a group and a year later she left her job with the Umbreits and became a full-time German Maiden organizer, being posted to the nearby small town of Monschau where she remained till early 1944.

Ilse Hirsch had suffered from a cough throughout her childhood; later this was to be diagnosed as TB and one of her lungs was collapsed to save her life. But in spite of her failing health, she applied for and was accepted into the Party and immediately her prospects brightened. In April, 1944, she was transferred to a new and better post in Aachen.

When Ilse Hirsch was sent to Hülchrath Castle in the winter of 1944 to prepare for 'Operation Carnival' she was 23 years old. She regarded herself as an *Idealistin*, who was not the least interested in the political doctrine of the National Socialist Workers' Party, but was concerned solely with the 'sense of community'; the working for a common cause. Later when asked why she, as a woman, had joined 'Operation Carnival', she stated, 'I did not join because I believed I was carrying out a mission for the Fuehrer. I was attracted by the adventure . . . the idea of carrying out a parachute jump.'

Yet this statement, which seems to indicate a carefree adventurous nature, contrasts strongly with her ice-cold, dedicated behaviour during the Operation when she actually saw for the first time that their intended victim had three small children and must have realized that if the assassination attempt were successful, she would not only be depriving a man of his life, but three children of their father.

THE ORGANIZATION OF THE WEREWOLVES
IN THE RHINELAND

COMMANDER: SS GENERAL GUTENBERGER
                (HQ Düsseldorf-Lohausen)
                        ↓

LIAISON OFFICER: SS COLONEL RADDATZ
                (Düsseldorf-Lohausen)
                        ↓

CO HÜLCHRATH: LT COL NEINHAUS
                (Hülchrath Castle)
                        ↓

TRAINING OFFICER: SS LT WENZEL
                (Hülchrath-Berlin)
                        ↓

WEREWOLF TEAMS: 5 MEN AND 1 WOMAN

RECRUITMENT AREAS: INTENDED EMPLOYMENT
Cologne   Army Group B (FM
Essen   Model). Between Schmid-
Dusseldorf[1]   theim and Cleves

[1] I.e. party districts centered on these towns.

In fact, Ilse Hirsch was a hardened and dedicated member of the Nazi Party, who, though not concerned with its ideology, obeyed its dictates without question. She would not hesitate for one moment to kill someone if it were in the interests of the 'cause'. A fanatic, in other words, and a brave one to boot.

VI

Ilse took an instant dislike to Lt Herbert Wenzel, who informed her that he was the chief training officer of the strange new unit to which Raddatz had assigned her. The unit was made up of both male and female personnel, some dressed in civilian clothes and others in uniform without badges of rank or identification save for the silver runes of the SS. In the two days she spent in one of the bare rooms in the turreted keep of the castle, Ilse had little contact with Wenzel. But during the long hazardous drive to the village of Galhausen near the Belgian town of St Vith which had finally been evacuated by the Americans after a spirited defence under General Bruce Clarke,[1] she got to know the young lieutenant a little better.

Not that Wenzel gave much away. He told her a little of his life story as they jolted over the shell-cratered *pavé* Eifel roads towards their destination, but he did so without that openness which Germans expect of each other. He had been born in Africa and had lived with an uncle on a farm in former German South-West Africa (after 1918 part of South Africa) till the outbreak of the war. Then he had fled to Germany to join the Army, leaving his family to be interned by the South Africans. Because of his fluent knowledge of English, he had been called up for a special undercover formation, *das Regiment Brandenburg*

[1] The defence of St Vith during the Battle of the Bulge is one of the epics of the Battle, but due to the unfortunate circumstance that the best part of the US 106th Infantry Division surrendered outside the town it is one that is hardly known to the general public.

The 'Brandenburgers', as they called themselves, were a small select group of soldiers who had spent many years abroad and because of their linguistic ability were used to carry out sabotage and similar operations behind enemy lines. Some time in 1943, Wenzel told her that he had volunteered with other members of the Regiment to join Major Otto Skorzeny's commando troops, then forming in Berlin.

Wenzel claimed that he had been part of that force which had rescued the imprisoned Mussolini from his surprised Italian guards. He told her that thereafter he had gone with Skorzeny to fight partisans in Jugoslovia, finally leaving the Commando in 1944 for a posting to Eltiville near Mainz, from where in October, 1944, he had been sent to Gutenberger. Even though Wenzel leaned over and showed Ilse Hirsch a pass signed with the sinking scrawl 'Obersturmbannführer O. Skorzeny', she knew that he was lying to her. He had told her that he had spent his whole life till 1939 outside Germany, yet he spoke with the guttural accent of a man who had been born and bred in North Germany; even the slight lisp that marred his speech could not hide that. Later, too, she was to find out that his English was not so fluent as he claimed; in fact, as far as she could judge, he made elementary mistakes, which he certainly should not have made if he had spent his whole life in an English-speaking community.

Ilse Hirsch soon gave up trying to discover the real Herbert Wenzel and her dislike of him grew as their training continued. Later all she could tell the British interrogation officers was that he was a 'secretive man, who thought slowly, couldn't act quickly and wasn't particularly suitable to be the leader of our mission.'

It was not till many years later that Ilse Hirsch began to realize how cunning Wenzel had really been, for he had presented a different face to everyone at Hülchrath. For Neinhaus he had been 'competent'; Gutenberger had found him 'efficient and quick'; Heidorn felt he was 'authoritarian, but had an amazing faculty for crossing country' (and this was high praise from a man who had risked his life three times to smuggle German agents through the American lines in the Eifel).

He had also given everyone with whom he had come into contact a different story of his background. Gutenberger thought he had 'come from the Skorzeny organization . . . probably from the Brandenbergers'; yet soon after he had made his first appearance at Hülchrath, he came to duty one day wearing the black uniform of an SS lieutenant in the *Panzertruppe*.[1]

Hennemann remarked, too, on the fact that although he wore the badges of an officer, he insisted on sleeping in the same quarters as the NCOs—very strange behaviour indeed for a German officer. Ilse Hirsch had the impression that he had passed the Abitur[2] and had spent several terms at a university; yet Heidorn noted while they were hiding out together on the farm after the murder, that Wenzel knew 'his way around a farmyard and had obviously had plenty of experience with horses', an observation confirmed by the farmer.

While Wenzel and Ilse Hirsch drove to St Vith to Gutenberger's advanced headquarters, General Gutenberger himself was still at his main headquarters in the bunker at Düsseldorf-Lohausen, a suburb of the fashionable Rhenish city, waiting for his orders to leave for Belgium. It was while he was waiting to go that he received a telephone call from Himmler.

Himmler was soon to take part in the Ardennes Offensive himself. For the first time the Fuehrer had granted him the opportunity to exercise his powers of leadership in battle; in the first days of January he was to launch a surprise diversionary attack on the Franco-American line in Alsace near Strasbourg. But although he was excited by this new challenge, he did not forget his routine duties nor his anger at the shocking way the Party officials had acted at Aachen, thus allowing traitors like the new chief burgomaster of the city to spread

---

[1] Tank Corps.
[2] The German high school leaving certificate, entitling the possessor to go to university.

poison among the German Nation with the aid of the enemy press.

The new responsibility had caused his nervous stomach pains to increase and, without waiting for Gutenberger to explain the situation, the Reichsführer irritably reprimanded him for his lack of action in the 'Aachen matter'. He left no doubt in Gutenberger's mind that he wanted immediate action; the SS General knew just how the *Reichsheini*[1] would react if there were any more delays. 'But the situation at the front makes it very difficult to get anyone through, Herr Reichsführer,' Gutenberger protested hastily. 'With the offensive and—'

Himmler cut him short. 'Then send in your group by air, man,' he snapped and hung up.

Shaken by Himmler's tone, Gutenberger went into the outer office where Albath, Inspector of the local Security Police was waiting for him.

'It was Himmler,' he said. 'On about the Aachen affair.'

Albath nodded. Like most of the higher ranking officers and officials at Gutenberger's Düsseldorf HQ, he knew about the plan. He waited for Gutenberger to answer his unspoken question.

'He has ordered me to go ahead with it.'

Albath was a tough man. In these last years he had seen and heard things he dare not even tell his wife about, but all the same he felt himself shudder. Like Gutenberger he was a realist. If Gutenberger went ahead with the murder plan and the Allies won the war, he knew what the General's fate would be. At that moment he was glad he was not in Gutenberger's shoes.

Nor was interest in Oppenhoff and his fellow town councillors confined to the German High Command, for the Americans were also becoming increasingly concerned about their German administrators. On the first day of the new year Capt Padover, head of one of the 12th Army Group's psychological warfare

[1] A derogatory name used among Party members for Himmler.

teams, was ordered to report to General Bradley's head-quarters, in an hotel in the centre of Luxemburg City.

Like the citizens of Aachen and its American occupiers, the Luxemburgers and their American liberators had been badly scared by the Ardennes Offensive. But now that Montgomery in the north and Patton in the south were moving in on the German salient and it was clear that the steam had gone out of the enemy attack, a new mood of confidence was to be found everywhere in the capital. Saul Padover with his trained nose for 'atmosphere' told himself that it was more than just confidence, it was a mood of aggressive retribution.

His feeling was confirmed when his chief, Col Powell, told him his new assignment. He was to take a team and investigate 'the situation in Aachen'. Way back in October one of the editors of the American Army newspaper *Stars and Stripes* had dressed as a private soldier and allowed himself to be sent to the city as a reinforcement. After spending some time there unobserved, he had returned to his office and written a very critical article about the way in which the 1st Army was treating the Germans in the city; in his opinion, the First was being 'too soft on the Krauts'.

The First Army had pressed Eisenhower to bring charges against the officer responsible, but the scandal had blown over. Now, however, things had changed. General Bradley, commander of the 12th Army Group, had been caught off his guard by the Ardennes Offensive and he was in no mood to tolerate any soft treatment of the Germans, military or otherwise. They should be punished and he had no objection to the efforts of his '*sykewar*' people in this field. As Capt Padover was to write later 'Psychological Warfare was interested in finding out what was going on in the city because there were redolent rumours that affected public opinion. First Army had not encouraged any investigation, but during the Rundstedt offensive Aachen was taken over by the Ninth Army which had no objections to an inquiry. On the contrary, it welcomed one.' Capt Padover, who spoke fluent German, set off with his two

Lieutenants, Sweet and Gittler, to make a 'thorough survey' of the city as Col Powell had ordered. They found a house in a ruined street which had walls and a roof, but was without gas, electricity, running water or a lavatory, and there they settled in and began their task of investigating Aachen. It was not easy. Not only did the three men have the harsh winter conditions to contend with, they also found that after five thirty in the evening, which was curfew time for the Germans, it was not wise to venture on the streets, since trigger-happy MPs fired first and asked questions afterwards.

It did not take them long, however, to learn that a storm was raging behind the scenes in the American Military Government offices located in the old Suermondt Museum. It revolved around the basic question of whether former Nazis and other undesirables should be retained in office, because they were the only German civilians prepared and able to run the stricken city.

According to Padover, the Military Government was split into three groups. A majority supported the Oppenhoff administration; their business, they said coldly, was 'efficiency' and not politics. A minority, consisting of the deputy MGO and two lieutenants, urged the elimination of Nazis from the Administration. Somewhere between the two was Major Jones, the Military Government Officer himself, who knew little about Germany and nothing of the German language and was perfectly neutral on the subject of the Nazis. To begin with, Padover went to work on Major Jones, who, because he had not appointed the original city administration, felt that his 'hands were clean'. But Jones did not respond to Padover's pleas to get rid of Oppenhoff and his group, even when the CIC supported the psychological warfare captain. 'In future, I shall be guided by three principles in making appointments,' he told Padover. 'First, a German must not be an ardent and active Nazi. Secondly, he must be respected in the community. Thirdly, he must be a man of character, and, of course, if he has character, he will be respected in the community.' However, Major Jones was not prepared to get rid of what an angry, excited Padover called 'the fifty-five Nazis in the administration'. 'Where,' he asked Padover, 'would you find competent people who are not Nazis?' and with that bit of unbeatable logic, the interview ended.

Padover began to broaden his investigation of the city. Soon he discovered, as he put it, that 'behind Oppenhoff and his administration was the Bishop of Aachen, and behind the Bishop stood Lt-Col S [Swoboda], the legal officer who was responsible for the selection of the *Oberbürgermeister* and his cabinet'.

From his CIC informants, Padover learned that Swoboda 'took no step without consulting the Bishop' whom he saw every day. In fact, as one MG officer, 'who approved neither of the Church in politics, nor of Nazis in office,' told him sardonically, 'Lt-Col Swoboda guards the Bishop like a mother hen.'

When Swoboda learned that Padover wanted to interview the Bishop, he 'raised hell' (as Padover wrote), but he could not stop the investigating officers who were empowered to carry out their work by 12th Army Group Headquarters itself. Swoboda supplied Padover with a letter explaining that Padover represented the 'propaganda division of the American Army' but Padover tore the letter up before he and his assistants set off for the interview.

The Bishop received the Americans in his living room and for a while they talked about things in general. Padover remarked that the Bishop's square, jowled face made him look like Winston Churchill.

The Bishop replied, unsmiling. 'I cannot help that'.

Swiftly Padover came to the point. He asked the Bishop about his first contact with the Americans, and he replied that the Nazi administration had ordered him to leave the city, but he had refused, hiding himself in the store, because 'a captain does not abandon his ship'. Then one day an American officer in a jeep had arrived in front of the Cathedral, just as he had come up for air from his cellar hiding-place in the store.

The Bishop had gone over to the American and said, 'I'm the Bishop of Aachen.' 'I'm a Catholic too,' the American had said and offered the Bishop a cigar. Then he drove him to the American headquarters.

'At this point in his conversation,' Padover wrote later, 'the Bishop became noticeably wary and cautious. He denied having had anything to do with the setting up of Aachen's city government. All he did, he said, was to mention Oppenhoff's name to Lt-Col S.' 'I do not make clique politics,' he said, 'I am neutral.'

Padover realized that the Bishop knew the city administration was under investigation and he guessed that it was Swoboda who had told him. Now the Bishop was obviously trying to protect the Church from any criticism that might be levelled at Oppenhoff. Bishop van der Velden was, Padover concluded, a very smart operator. All the same he fell into the trap of repeatedly referring to Oppenhoff's administration as 'we' and throughout the conversation he tried to defend the Church from any blame attached to Oppenhoff and at the same time to defend Oppenhoff himself. He was obviously anxious to make sure that Padover carried away a good impression of the chief burgomaster and his circle. 'Oppenhoff,' he assured Padover, 'is a brave man and a good lawyer. To be sure he is no model of virtue, but believe me he is a fine fellow. The other burgomasters, too, are splendid fellows. I know them personally, including Dr Pfeiffer, who is a Protestant.'

Inwardly Padover smiled. Protestants were human too! The Bishop was really being magnanimous!

'Their government is truly representative of the people; you must have confidence in him. You must leave things to him. If he says a person is reliable, believe me, he knows what he is talking about. A Nazi party badge in itself is meaningless. The deeper you go into Germany the more difficulty you will have in finding non-Nazis.'

It was dark when the American officers left. They left the bishop sitting alone in the dark room, smoking cigarette after cigarette.

For a while Padover was silent as the jeep rolled through the deserted, dangerous streets. He realized that the Bishop had put up an excellent performance. Occasionally there had been a gleam in the churchman's eyes behind the thick lenses almost as if he were asking, 'How am I doing?' And throughout the interview he had the sensation that van der Velden had been watching him shrewdly, appraising his every reaction to the Bishop's, words and shaping his answers accordingly. Yet, all the same, he had not believed one word the Bishop had said. He turned to Gittler and said, 'I guess we've got to go and see Oppenhoff next'.

The Oppenhoff interview was not a success. Right from the start things went wrong. He knew his administration was being investigated and he was not particularly pleased. The responsibility of his job, the danger attached to it and the constant harassment on the part of the Americans were getting on his nerves. As Padover entered he rose from behind his desk and greeted him 'in a tone in which vigour won over cordiality,' as Padover put it.

He did not waste time with Oppenhoff and he was not prepared to tolerate any side-tracking. Time and time again, he cut him off and made him come to the point, and the point was the employment of Nazis in his administration.

Admitting that his administration was criticized in the city because of its employment of men who had probably been party members, Oppenhoff said that this attitude on the part of 'certain elements' was outrageous. Why, they had even demanded that all Party members should be imprisoned! 'I hope that the American gentlemen will not commit such an injustice. Not all Nazis are guilty. In fact, only a few can be held responsible.'

He paused and drew a quick breath, 'There are three categories of Party members. Nazis by conviction. Nazis who changed their minds. Nazis who joined for business reasons. Only the first can be frowned upon. The other two classes can be safely employed in the highest positions. I have so employed them.'

Grimly Padover listened while the burgomaster plunged himself deeper and deeper in the mess. He had collaborated with the American Military Government, he told Padover, because he felt that a foreign occupation meant that for the next decade or so Germany would be spared political parties and trade unions. 'Thank God, that the Military Government and not the Germans will rule!'

Padover asked Oppenhoff to explain what he meant.

'There are three benefits that will be derived from Military Government,' he explained. 'First, the Americans will get to know the Germans. Secondly, government by the military will exclude all talkers, politicians and agitators. Thirdly, it will give us time to reconstruct our economy without interference from political parties and trade unions. It is, of course', he went on, confident that by now he had gained the support of the silent American officer, 'self-evident that the American Military Government will be wise enough to prevent the Germans from organizing parties and unions. Under no conditions,' he urged vehemently, 'must you Americans make any propaganda appeals to German workers. You must not promise them anything.'

He ended the conversation with a statement which was calculated to rouse the ire in a man of Padover's left-wing sentiments. In a voice that was rapidly becoming hoarse from so much talking, he told Padover, 'Europe is lost if Germany does not join the West to offset the Russians. If the United States only knew its own interests it would join Germany against the Soviet Asiatics!'

Padover got into his jeep fuming. As he wrote later, 'He spoke as if he were a citizen of a victorious nation and neither in his ideas nor his plans did he reveal any awareness that he was a member of a defeated country and an official of a conquered city.' Grimly, he promised himself that a few heads, American as well as German, would roll when 12th Army Group received his report.

Padover's report began, 'In the last three months a new

élite has emerged in Aachen, an élite made up of technicians, lawyers, engineers, businessmen, manufacturers and churchmen. This élite is shrewd, strong-willed and aggressive. It occupies every important job in the administration. Its leader is *Oberbürgermeister* Oppenhoff. Almost all the *Bürgermeisters* and key functionaries were chosen by him, and most of them think his way. Behind Oppenhoff is the Bishop of Aachen, a powerful figure with a subtlety of his own and a programme of the Church . . .

'Their strong point, especially in dealing with Americans, is that they are "anti-Nazi" or "non-Nazi". Their proof is that they never joined the Party. How and why did they escape Party membership? Oppenhoff says his circle did not depend on the Party because they were in the "free professions" or were closely connected with the Church and thus "could not join" . . .

'These leading officials kept out of the Wehrmacht because they volunteered their services to the war industry. Some of them, notably *Oberbürgermeister* Oppenhoff and his chief assistants Faust and Op de Hipt, sought "refuge" in Aachen's leading war plant . . . They all represent the upper middle-class; their earnings in the last ten years under Hitler have been high, ranging from seven thousand to two hundred thousand marks yearly, with the average of thirty thousand marks. None of them ever suffered under the Nazi régime—or ever, by word or deed, opposed it. The record shows that they prospered under Hitler.'

Padover continued his devastating report with a summary of the new administration's political attitude. 'The men around *Oberbürgermeister* Oppenhoff are not democratic-minded. They profess a marked distaste for the Weimar Republic, an abhorrence of party government, a dread of labour and a fearful suspicion of liberal movements. In varying degrees and tones, one or the other repeats the slogans and clichés of the Nazis and the "eternal Germans"—that Germany was "dishonoured" by the Versailles Treaty, that the latter was too harsh, that France is the permanent hereditary enemy, that Germany was betrayed when the Fourteen Points[1] were not kept, that the "poor" Reich is a "land without space" and must expand. They attribute the outbreak of war to these "evils" and charge the working class with being the main support of Hitler.'

Padover ended his report with a general comment on the situation in the American Military Government then functioning in occupied Germany. 'An MG team, therefore, will employ almost anybody it believes capable of putting a town on a functioning basis. Thus Nazi sympathizers, Party members, or German nationalists, are appointed by MG as the only available specialists. These specialists, who look extremely presentable and have professional backgrounds similar to those of MG officers, then place their like-minded friends in secondary positions. As a consequence, MG's initial indifference to the politics of the situation leads in the end to a political mess.'

With those words Capt Saul Padover made his last point. The report was ready for dispatch to higher headquarters. The 'political mess' would now rise the ladder of military responsibility until it reached the Supreme Commander, General Eisenhower. And Padover knew that Eisenhower, always sensitive to public opinion, would be forced to act, especially as Padover had organized powerful forces to back his recommendation[2]— *Oberbürgermeister Oppenhoff would have to go.*

Thus it was with a kind of tragic irony that on the same day that Saul Padover sent off his report recommending Oppenhoff's dismissal because of his alleged nationalistic and undemocratic attitude, another official communication reached SS General Gutenberger some sixty miles away. Brought by courier from Berlin, it came from Heinrich Himmler himself. It was brief and to the point.

[1] President Wilson's Fourteen Points of 1918.
[2] Notably Max Lerner, author, university teacher and editor of *PM*, who as a journalist at the 1st Army press camp in Spa had interested himself in the situation in Aachen.

When Gutenberger read it, his face went white and he was tempted to crumple it up and throw it away. But the waiting SS officer courier read his mind and told him that the Reichsfuhrer wanted the message back again. If he liked, he could, however, make a copy of it. Gutenberger nodded and turned to the waiting Raddatz. 'Take this down, please,' he ordered in a strained voice. Raddatz took out his pen and Gutenberger read the order. 'The Chief Burgomaster of Aachen has been sentenced to death. The sentence is to be carried out by W.'

IV
Operation Carnival

*'Losses can never be too high! They sow the
seeds of future greatness.'*

Adolf Hitler

I

The failure of the Ardennes Offensive increased General Gutenberger's sense of despair. His experiences behind the front had been nerve-racking. Once, visiting a Gestapo unit commanded by a Lt Schneider, from whom he hoped to get guides for the Aachen operation, he had come under artillery fire and publicly lost his nerve, throwing himself in a ditch in front of the contemptuous Gestapo men. The episode still rankled, for he knew that his own staff must know of it by now. By this time too, it was clear that it was only a matter of weeks— perhaps even only a week—before the *Amis* recovered from their set-back in the Ardennes and then started pushing deeper into Germany. Within a month they could be over the Rhine and then he knew that all was lost. The war would be over and he would have to pay the price of being on the losing side. Yet it was under these circumstances that he was expected to order the murder of the chief burgomaster of *Ami*-occupied Aachen; and he was quite clear in his own mind—whatever Raddatz and the others of his staff thought to the contrary—that the victorious *Amis* would regard the assassination as murder.

But although an inner voice told him repeatedly to keep away from the Aachen affair, or 'Operation Chief Burgomaster' as it was now being openly called in his Düsseldorf-Lohausen headquarters, he knew too that Himmler would not tolerate further delay. He was close enough to the top Party Leaders to realize that there was a new, almost nihilistic, feeling reigning in Berlin. It was as if the Party bosses knew that the 'Thousand Year Empire', as they once so proudly called the Third Reich, was about to fall apart and were prepared to drag everything and everyone down with them into the last bloody holocaust. He had no illusions about what would happen to him if he failed to carry out the assignment Himmler had given him.

Himmler was not the ruthless, cold-blooded sadist the enemy-press made him out to be, Karl Gutenberger knew that; the *Reichsheini* did not delight in cruelty for the sake of cruelty.

He was simply indifferent to it. With fanatical naive faith in the 'German cause', he would simply pick up a telephone, issue an order and forget the whole matter, feeling neither pleasure nor displeasure at the knowledge that he had just sentenced one of his loyal subordinates to be 'taken care of'. Gutenberger felt he understood Himmler's mentality completely. Even if everyone else in Germany knew they had lost the war, the *Reichsfuehrer SS* would still believe that the Third Reich had a chance and punish anyone who failed to subscribe to that belief.[1]

So in the first week of February, 1945 Gutenberger set about the completion of the Aachen assignment. While the rumble of the Allied guns in the Eifel grew louder and louder, giving a foretaste of the offensive soon to come, he gave orders to Wenzel to assemble the murder team for 'Operation Chief Burgomaster' at Hülchrath.

Wenzel was pleased with his new assignment. He did not like the 'mass operations' of the front and he was glad to get back from the Ardennes fiasco, in which he had played a spectator's role, although many of his old comrades had taken part in Skorzeny's *Trojan Horse Operations*,[2] which would have been right up his own particular street.

Now he was back in Hülchrath and the quiet life of the rear echelon, with Hella, the plump blonde SS telephonist, waiting for him expectantly every time he managed to get to Gutenberger's HQ at Düsseldorf and his actress girl-friend at Erkelenz writing him passionate love-letters every other day urging him to come and see her as soon as possible.

At the same time he knew that his quiet days in the 'cushy billet' at Hülchrath were numbered. Either the Allies would take the place soon or he would have to lead the team to Aachen, risking his neck in a venture which he felt would not influence

[1] Himmler was, however, already being forced to consider the possibility of having to negotiate with the Allies under the influence of SS Secret Service Chief General Schellenberg.

[2] Sneaking behind the American line in US uniforms in order to carry out sabotage operations.

the course of the war one bit. We do not know what passed through Herbert Wenzel's mind when he realized that he would have to go ahead with 'Operation Chief Burgomaster'. Outwardly he seemed pleased, but perhaps that was because the planning of the operation ensured that he stayed a little while longer in the comfortable, safe harbour of the rear echelon. None of his fellow conspirators felt that he was an 'enthusiastic party-member' or 'overly interested' in the operation, when they were questioned by the British security officers after the war. For them he was a 'man of mystery' who was often absent in the Eifel, seemed to have direct contact with Pruetzmann in Berlin, but otherwise went about planning the operation in a 'routine, deliberate way' without any particular excitement or enthusiasm.

Perhaps Wenzel thought that the operation would give him an opportunity for disappearing and thus saving his neck. But whatever his reactions were, Wenzel kept them to himself, the only indication of the way his mind was working at that time being the great care he took to conceal his movements and contacts from his superiors as well as from his fellow conspirators. Wenzel, it seems, was playing both sides of the field.

In the first week of February, 1945, he conducted a tour of the school at Hülchrath. By now the Werewolf organization was beginning to take shape. From Berlin had come the orders to break the fifty young men and women receiving training up into six-man teams. Each team would consist of four men, one boy and a woman. The boy and woman members would act as scouts, because, as Pruetzmann stated, 'young boys and women rouse little suspicion in the occupied territories'. The men would be divided into two groups of two, each man ready to carry out the duties of the other in case one was captured or killed.

As Wenzel walked round the school that afternoon, looking at his youngsters practising their deadly handiwork with youthful dedication—throwing their captured British mills bombs, taking *Panzerfausts* apart with their eyes blindfolded while they looked for stoppages, flinging each other all over the courtyard in unarmed combat, he began to plan his team.

The women member was an obvious choice—Ilse Hirsch. He didn't like her, and he guessed she didn't like him. With her pasty face, sullen hard mouth and double chin, she was not the type he liked to go to bed with. He liked his girls blonde, nubile and easy-going. You might win a war with women like the Hirsch, but you didn't sleep with them. All the same, she was ideal for the job on hand; she was tough, hard as nails, dedicated, and knew the area like the back of her hand. She'd make the best female scout.

As his second-in-command he realized he would have to take someone who was experienced in the use of weapons, since he or his second-in-command would have to carry out the assassination. He needed an experienced soldier. In the end he decided to pick his second-in-command from the handful of SS instructors. He picked SS Sergeant Josef Leitgeb, a broad-shouldered, blond Austrian from Innsbruck who was in his early thirties. Leitgeb had joined the SS in Austria long before Hitler had annexed the country and as a result of a brawl with an Austrian anti-Nazi group he had been forced to flee his native country, losing his citizenship as a consequence. He escaped to Germany, where he first joined the Austrian Legion, a para-military formation made up of Austrian Nazis like himself. But after the *Anschluss* he had transferred to the *Allgemeine SS*, the pre-war Black Guard unit, which not only supplied the guards for the newly-opened concentration camps but also the nucleus for the wartime *Waffen SS*. Leitgeb had had 'Schwein',[1] as he himself was the first to admit. During the course of the war he had neither been sent to a concentration camp where even the strongest weakened after a while, nor to the front with the *Waffen SS*, to die violently in some nameless blizzard-ridden Russian forest. Instead he had spent a pleasant war in a headquarters job pretending to be a radio operator, though both

[1] 'To have a pig'. German expression for 'to be lucky'.

Wenzel and Captain Renner, Gutenberger's radio man, knew that the burly slow-thinking Austrian was hopeless when it came to contacting anyone by radio.

All the same Leitgeb was tough and without nerves, taking things as they came, in that easy-going unthinking Austrian way of his. Besides, Wenzel liked the way the Austrian treated the women; it indicated a man who was self-confident and was plagued little by scruples or doubts. A few drinks, a little flattery in that soft, insinuating German of his, and the girl would be on her back in some hotel bedroom with her skirts up over her head. Wenzel had been out a couple of times with the Austrian and had admired the way the latter had overcome all his female partner's scruples, twisting even the most experienced of women around his little finger. Leitgeb, he told himself, was a man of resources and little imagination; it was a good combination for the job they had to do. And, as events turned out, his estimate of Leitgeb's character and capabilities was completely correct.

But what about the other scout—the boy that Pruetzmann had suggested should go along with every six-man team? On that same afternoon that he inspected the school, Wenzel went back to his office in the second floor of the keep and began to look through the personal records of the Hitler Youth members presently under training. Outside, NCOs bellowed orders and every now and again there would be the ugly persistent sound of someone trying to start a truck in the bitterly cold weather. Having looked through the files, Wenzel went to the ice-patterned window which was frozen up on both sides of the pane, opened it and called down to one of the NCO's in the courtyard below, 'Send up Erich Morgenschweiss!'

'*Jawohl, Herr Untersturmbannfuehrer!*' the NCO bellowed back and stamped away over the hard frozen snow to fetch the sixteen-year-old youth. Wenzel had decided on the fourth member of the murder team.

Erich Morgenschweiss had been born in the mining village of Merkstein just outside Aachen in 1928. His father was a miner, just as his father before him had been and probably his father too. In Merkstein every able-bodied man went into the *Puett*,[1] the group of mines which lay in the valley that ran down from the end of the village. But Erich Morgenschweiss, with his carefully-arranged, wavy blond hair and his delicate features, had never felt any desire to follow in his father's foot-steps. For Morgenschweiss the mine meant danger (not a family in the village had escaped losing one of its members in the two mining disasters which had struck the mines in the twentieth century) and dirt; the dirt was deeply engrained in his father's ears and torn knuckles, and no amount of pitbaths could ever erase those dark particles of coal from under the old man's skin.

Thus when it was time for Erich Morgenschweiss to leave school and go to work, he had refused to go in the mines, selecting instead a further year in school at an Aachen college of commerce. It was his first attempt to get away from Merkstein and the *Puett*.

His second was his decision to join the Hitler Youth. The 'movement' provided the glamour and adventure sorely missing in the small mining village. Erich was soon a dedicated member of the Hitler Youth and it was not long before he had worked himself up to patrol leader. Proudly wearing the coveted patrol leader's lanyard he would carry out his nightly patrol of the local cafés and inns to check whether teenagers were present without Party permission with a deadly serious mien that caused secret laughter among his friends. In the late summer of 1944, as the Americans pushed closer to the German frontier, Erich was evacuated from Merkstein. Separated from his parents, with no school to attend, he decided to join the Hitler Youth as a full-time youth leader. He applied and was accepted, and in November 1944 was sent to Schloss Hülchrath to be trained for the new secret guerrilla organization.

Though usually loud-mouthed and boastful, Morgenschweiss was quiet enough when he reported to Wenzel that afternoon.

[1] Pit.

Politely he tapped on the door and when Wenzel called to him to enter, he opened the door, clicked his heels together and flinging out his hand, cried '*Heil Hitler, Herr Untersturmbann-fuehrer!*'

'*Heil Hitler!*' Wenzel replied, a little wearily. He could not quite get used to the term being part and parcel of military life. It was bad enough hearing it all the time in government offices, but now ever since the attempt on the Fuehrer's life in July, 1944, the Military had been forced to use it too; it was sometimes a little too much for him.

'Sit down, Morgenschweiss.' In private he called him *Fusschweiss*[1] and sometimes he was afraid he would address the boy with the name.

'Thank you, *Herr Untersturm*,' Morgenschweiss said and sitting down, wiped the sweat from his forehead. He had been called from the athletics period and he was still sweating in spite of the bitter cold outside. Carefully he pushed his hair into place, and waited for Wenzel to speak.

'You know about the Aachen operation?' Wenzel asked.

'Yes, when I was at Lohausen as a messenger they talked about the job. And Herr Stubenrauch[2] said something about killing the chief burgomaster of Aachen.'

Wenzel nodded and thought how lousy their security was. Everyone and his son seemed to know about the operation. But he did not reprove the boy. He knew that Morgenschweiss was a favourite of Gutenberger's and he did not want to run foul of the SS Police General. It could be dangerous. 'He is a traitor and must be liquidated,' Morgenschweiss said somewhat hesitantly.

'Yes,' Wenzel agreed. 'Now you know the Aachen area?'

---

[1] Morgenschweiss means 'morning sweat'. Behind his back the other male members of the Aachen team often called him *Fusschweiss*—'foot sweat'. Heidorn called him *Schweissfuss*.

[2] Stubenrauch, a former counter-espionage man who belonged to the Gestapo and gave occasional lectures at Hülchrath, had mentioned the planned operation to Morgenschweiss early in January.

108

'I went to the commercial school there, and Merkstein, where I come from, is only a few kilometres away.'

Wenzel nodded thoughtfully, as if he were hearing the details for the first time, although he knew them already from Morgenschweiss's personal file. He wondered whether he could entrust his life to this callow, loud-mouthed boy. Morgenschweiss had his advantages, of course. He was enthusiastic and, like most of the boys in the Castle, he would not hesitate to kill if ordered to; they had been trained from the day they had joined the *Jungvolk*[1] to believe anyone who resisted the will of the Fuehrer did not deserve to live anyway.

But all the same, Morgenschweiss was not the kind to whom one would entrust a secret. He talked too much and too loudly. The other two, Hirsch and Leitgeb, could be relied on to keep silent about the operation. But not Morgenschweiss. If he were told that he was to be a member of the team for Aachen, half Düsseldorf would know about it next day; the boy simply had to show off.

Wenzel sighed. It was a difficult decision to make. Yet he needed another scout and Morgenschweiss was the best of a bad bunch. He made up his mind.

'I want you to come along on the Aachen operation.'

Morgenschweiss' face beamed. '*Herr Untersturm Wenzel*,' he said enthusiastically, rolling the 'l' of the other man's name in that typical Rhenish way of his, 'many thanks for this opportunity—this *great* opportunity!'

Wenzel nodded and dismissed him. He felt suddenly that he deserved a trip to Lohausen to see the plump Hella with her thick lips and eager appetite for bed.

On 20 February the last two members of the six-man team arrived at the Castle, the guides Heidorn and Hennemann, provided by the Gestapo Lt Schneider, who privately had told an intimate when he had heard what job they were to undertake, 'I'm keeping *my* nose out of the whole business!'

[1] The most junior youth movement, something like the 'cubs'.

The two guides were former border policemen who had been enrolled in the SS in the middle years of the war; once the Allies reached Belgium in the summer of 1944 they had been employed as '*Frontläufer*' or 'front runners'—men and women who knew the border area so intimately that they were capable of guiding agents, agitators, saboteurs and the like back and forth through enemy lines. Hennemann, the older of the two, was very experienced in this dangerous business[1] and boasted of having made some thirty trips and of winning Germany's highest award for bravery in the process—the Knight's Cross of the Iron Cross. Privately, Georg Heidorn, his fellow guide, did not believe that the older man had completed so many missions. He had done three himself, including one hair-raising journey through the *Ami* lines in the Ardennes to take a French saboteur as far as the American-occupied Belgian town of Eupen, and he knew how they ate into a man's courage and nerves. All the same he knew that Hennemann had been through the *Ami* lines seven or eight times in these last few months while they had been working together under the command of Lt Schneider and once he had been dropped by parachute behind the front, gaining the coveted close-combat badge[2] during that particular mission.

Both men had been in the border police before the war and had served in the Aachen area then and during the war. As a result they knew the frontier, and especially the Dreiländereck, intimately. And both were careful men, who in spite of their dangerous jobs, valued their lives and were not prepared to throw them away on any hair-brained scheme.

Hennemann, the older of the two, looked like the traditional village idiot. He had a heavy hanging jaw and narrow forehead

[1] Not only because of the normal dangers inherent in a front-line situation, but also because the *Frontläufer* often wore civilian clothes and ran the risk of being shot as a spy if caught.

[2] A metal badge worn on the left breast indicating that the wearer had been engaged in hand-to-hand combat with the enemy or at least involved in close-range fighting.

and when he wasn't speaking, his mouth often hung open to reveal his ugly, yellow teeth. But in spite of his appearance he was an energetic, brave, determined man, who was well aware of the advantage his face gave him when he was working behind enemy lines; no one would take him for a spy or saboteur.

Georg Heidorn, with deep-set eyes and bold chin, looked very much the man of action. Yet in fact, it was Heidorn and not Hennemann, who was first to get cold feet when he learned from Wenzel what was expected of him. Right from the start, the junior guide began to think of ways of getting out of the foolhardy operation which he felt could only end in death for them all.

In the last week of February Gutenberger drove down to Hülchrath to confer for the last time with the conspirators. As he drove along the narrow winding Route Number One from his headquarters in Lohausen, he knew the end was not far off. On the horizon, the pink flashes of the Allied barrage broke up the leaden grey of the winter sky at regular intervals; and every now and again his big black Horch had to move into the centre of the pitted road to let pass yet another pathetic column of horse-drawn wagons—'treks', as the locals called them—filled with old men, women and children and their possessions, fleeing from the advancing *Amis*.

The six of them were waiting for him when he arrived at the Castle. Wenzel brought them to their feet and while all of them stood rigidly to attention, he reported at the top of his voice.

Gutenberger touched his peaked cap and then told them to sit down. Then he nodded to Raddatz. *'Standartenfuehrer!'*

Raddatz strode into the middle of the room. For a moment he did not speak but ran his eyes round the pale faces of the waiting conspirators. In spite of the fact he was in no mood for humour, Karl Gutenberger smiled to himself. The little man savoured such moments; he liked the power that this captive audience gave him. *'Na, alte Freund'*, he told himself, staring at Raddatz's back, 'one day when they let you out of jail, you'll be doing this all the time. You'll be back in the schools, teaching the *ABC Schützen*.'[1]

Raddatz began, 'The chief burgomaster has been sentenced to death by the People's Court in Berlin[2] because he has proved himself a traitor to the German People.'

He paused and let the information sink in. Gutenberger, staring at his back, was a little shocked at his subordinate's nerve. Raddatz was an *Akademiker*—an educated man. Surely he didn't believe that stuff about the Aachen burgomaster being sentenced to death by a court? Yet he had said the words with conviction, as if he really believed them.[3]

Raddatz spoke again. 'The highest officer in the Reich, Reichsführer Himmler himself, has ordered that we carry out the death sentence. The operation is to be called Operation Carnival!' He paused as if he expected a comment, a burst of laughter. After all there was a kind of supreme irony about the choice of cover name. The only kind of carnival going to be held in the last spring of the war was that involving violent death. Whoever had picked the name had been a cynic. But there was no reaction from his audience. Perhaps their simple minds did not run to such subtleties. He sighed at having to deal with such people and continued. Quickly he sketched in the operation. Because they were threatened by an Allied push through the Eifel, it had been decided that the parachute drop would start from the Luftwaffe airfield at Hildesheim near Brunswick and not from Dusseldorf. There Luftwaffe Squadron 252 had captured enemy planes which would be used to carry them safely to their objective. However, recent reconnaissance had shown that Aachen was heavily defended by anti-aircraft batteries. As a result they would not drop over the city itself

[1] 'The ABC Rifles', a name given to schoolchildren in their first year in Germany.

[2] After the war a search was made through the records of this court. No documents were ever found pertaining to Oppenhoff.

[3] During his university years, Raddatz had actually studied civil law for a couple of terms and must have known that the execution of a death sentence involved more than a letter to that effect from Himmler.

but inside Belgium where the *Amis* would not expect any German agents to land.

While the others listened attentively Raddatz explained to Heidorn and Hennemann the planned route. They would drop near the little Belgian village of Gemmenich in the Dreiländereck and from there it would be their job to guide the group round the outskirts of the city until they reached their base camp at the Pelzerturm, an area of woods and open pastures close to the Belgian-German frontier near the road to Eupen. Hennemann and Heidorn both nodded their approval and understanding, but all the while Heidorn's mind was reeling. He had been with the police and Gestapo long enough to know that you just did not condemn someone to death like this. Even if the burgomaster were an enemy of the people and Himmler had ordered the death sentence passed on him, there had to be documents, forms, written details.

He stole a glance at his fellow guide. But Hennemann's heavy-set face revealed nothing. He seemed to believe the rubbish that Raddatz was telling them. Suddenly Heidorn shivered. It was as if someone had drawn an icy finger down the small of his back. He was afraid of what was to come.

When Raddatz finished his briefing, General Gutenberger beckoned the two guides to come forward to look at the map. After explaining that Wenzel and Leitgeb would execute the Himmler order and Hirsch and Morgenschweiss would do the scouting in Aachen itself, he asked the two guides to indicate the escape route in case the group was broken up after the execution.

Hennemann, as the senior guide, quickly traced in the route they would take. Leaving Aachen, they would travel cross-country, plunging into the deep woods of the Eifel, avoiding inhabited places wherever possible. During the daytime they would hide and rest in a number of lonely foresters' houses he knew of behind the enemy lines, assuming that these would probably now be empty or abandoned due to the fighting. At night they would attempt to cover as much ground as possible by means of forced marches. If they were challenged, they would let the woman do the talking. However, if the *Amis* insisted on looking at their documents, they would produce the faked papers supplied by Stubenrauch and pretend to be workers from the *Todt-Organization*.[1] Their final assembly point after the deed would be Gut Hombusch, a lonely farm set high on a wooded hill near the village of Mechernich.

Schneider's group, to which Hennemann and Heidorn had belonged had once occupied this farmhouse but now it was only occupied by Baron Solemacher and his servants. It would make an ideal hiding place, where they could rest for a few days, completely cut off from the outer world, before they commenced the last lap of their journey.

When Hennemann had finished, Gutenberger nodded his approval, then moved into the centre of the room. 'I must warn you,' he said 'that this operation is top secret. You know the penalty for revealing such a secret to any unauthorized persons?'

There was a mumble of acknowledgement. Gutenberger indicated Wenzel should come forward. From his briefcase, he took the money, thick wads of brand new Belgian Francs and Allied Marks.[2] He handed it to Wenzel. 'Divide that among your group.'

Wenzel's eyes widened for a moment when he saw the money but he took it without any comment and began to divide it among the group, giving each member from one to two thousand Belgian francs and a large sum in Allied marks.

Politely Gutenberger waited till Wenzel was finished and then he remarked casually, almost as if he were commenting

[1] The German Labour Organization, made up of youngsters and old men, not fit for military service, which had done a lot of work on the frontier emplacements in the winter of '44 and early '45.

[2] When the Allies entered Germany they produced their own 'military marks', intended solely for use in their own installations. It is not known whether the money Gutenberger gave the conspirators was genuine or whether it was forged by the expert concentration camp forgers working for the Nazis under duress.

on the state of the weather, 'Operation Carnival starts in six days.' And with that he left the room.

II

The survivors of Operation Carnival had little to say about the events of the next few days when they were questioned about them years later, first by the British Intelligence men and then by the German public prosecutor. For all of them, there seemed to be a certain dreamlike quality about those early days of March and nothing very much is known about what happened during this period.

Although Gutenberger himself returned to Hülchrath one last time and saw the whole team in a kind of final celebration, wishing each and every one 'lots of success' at the end of the evening, he seemed surprised to find them a few days later in the antechamber of his office which had been evacuated to Schloss Flick near the village of Kettwig in the Ruhr. 'What are you doing here?' he asked when he saw Wenzel. Then, before Wenzel could answer, he had ushered him into his office, and the next day the six members of the team found themselves being driven in a police truck towards the north German town of Hildesheim.

It was the same at Hildesheim. No one seemed to know anything about them or their mission, yet when Wenzel picked up the phone at the little hotel near the station and called the duty room of the local airfield, a voice answered, 'Wenzel? Yes, we know all about you.'

Some might explain the vagueness of the conspirators' recollections by the confused state of Germany at the time. In the first week of March an armoured reconnaissance team from the US 1st Army had seized the bridge at Remagen. General Eisenhower ordered the bridgehead built up and a few days later four American divisions started to push across the Rhine.

At the same time British and American bombers began to seal off the Ruhr industrial area, blasting the exit roads, railways and bridges leading out of the Ruhr preparatory to Montgomery's 'set-piece' crossing of the Rhine. Everywhere it was clear that Germany's defeat was only a matter of weeks away. *Der Endkampf*, the final battle, had begun.

The group was not in particularly good health as they waited at their hotel in Hildesheim. Both Heidorn and Hennemann were sick with a high fever and pneumonia; Leitgeb and Wenzel felt physically exhausted and Ilse Hirsch's cough seemed to be getting steadily worse. Even Morgenschweiss was dispirited, appreciating for the first time what he had committed himself to.

Perhaps we are expecting too much in trying to establish the feelings of the six conspirators. The Third Reich was a gangster Empire whose rulers behaved like the actors in a second-grade film. It was a world in which nothing was too fantastic to happen; in which there no 'normal' motives and no 'normal' feelings. Lies, bribes, blackmail, faked papers, treachery and violence were part and parcel of the daily routine. The Werewolves, brought up in this extraordinary world, were prepared to murder a man whom they did not know, at the behest of an official whom they had never seen, without the slightest qualm. In all their statements after the war, there is not one word of doubt, indecision, fear, or regret. *Befehl ist Befehl*, 'Orders are Orders', they would repeat to their interrogators, as if that phrase would explain everything. And that was that.

It was a warm evening for the time of the year and the room in which they found themselves at the airfield, with its tightly-fitting blackout shutters, was hot and smelled of sweat. Ilse Hirsch held her hand underneath her nose and smelled the perfume of the soap with which she had washed herself carefully and thoroughly before they had left the Hotel Hotopp. The perfume took her mind off the odour of the crew-room which threatened to make her sick, although she kept telling herself it was just nerves like Morgenschweiss' frequent visits to the nearby toilet.

She looked around the dingy room with its lockers, their doors scarred from being forced open so many times when their owners had taken off never to return, and its fly-blown official photograph of enemy bombers. One of them had been pointed out by the Captain as the plane that would fly them to their destination. He had called it a Flying Fortress. She recognized the plane from the raids on Aachen and the newsreels she had seen where the *Ami* planes had come falling dramatically out of the sky in their dozens, engines on fire, smoke pouring from their tails and great black lumps breaking off their wings. She wondered how the *Luftwaffe* had managed to get the enemy plane down in one piece.

An officer strode into the crew-room. It was the Oberleutnant she had seen with Wenzel the first time they had come up to the field. He nodded to the SS officer and walked over to Hennemann. Whispering a few words to the guide, he gave him the package with the money for the renegade English captain who was working for the Germans. Once Hennemann had buried it beneath a certain border stone on the Belgian-German frontier, its position would be radioed to the Englishman so he could pick it up as a reward for his treachery. Ilse Hirsch watched as Hennemann stowed away the $5,000 packet and thought about the English traitor. What had he done to earn that kind of money? It was a small fortune. She looked at her fellow conspirators. In spite of their pale faces she knew none of them would ever turn traitor. They had all sworn an oath to stick together and promised that any traitor in their midst would not live very long to enjoy the fruits of his treachery.

A short while later they received their sandwiches and coffee in flasks and were told to go along the covered passage to the next building. It was the parachute shop, a tall echoing hanger that was so brightly lit that Ilse's eyes watered a little after the smoke and poor lighting of the crew room. Her nose wrinkled. She could not identify the smell, but it seemed to be the floor polish. For a moment she wondered what they would be doing with floor polish in a place like this. Then it was her turn to collect her chute. A bored *Luftwaffe* soldier dragged the chute and harness from the shelf and threw it on the well-scrubbed wooden counter in front of her. Picking it up with a grunt, she followed the others outside.

Out of the half-light loomed the gigantic shape of the captured American bomber and as she got closer to it, bowed under the weight of the parachute and harness, she could see new metal patches everywhere patching up the fabric. The crew were lined up on the other side of the aircraft, with their backs to her, urinating. She looked away and wondered why they had not relieved themselves before. She did not know that a full bladder at high altitude could cause agonies of pain for anyone sitting in a seat for hours on end.

The crew swung themselves up into the aircraft, making it, with their years of practice, look very easy. The Werewolf team followed, but rather more clumsily. When they were all in, the little green lamp in the control room, at the far side of the runway, began to flicker. The big plane started to shake and the noise of the engines rose deafeningly. The Fortress rolled forward, its speed quickly increasing. Up in his cockpit the skipper drove it up an invisible ramp, as if forcing it—by a sheer effort of will—to leave the earth. In a moment they were gaining height, flying up into the clouds and darkness.

The time was nine o'clock on the evening of 20 March, 1945. In another couple of hours they would be over the dropping zone.

III

It did not take Ilse long to find out the name and the address of the *Ami* burgomaster of Aachen.

As soon as she arrived in the ruined city, she went straight away to her old apartment in the Hasselholzerweg. It was a stupid thing to do. She had lived in the apartment for six months in 1944 while she had been employed as German Maiden organizer in the city. Someone could have recognized and reported her to the police; by this time the *Amis* had already set up their own German police force, composed of elderly civilians, whose badge of office was a wooden club and an armband. But fortunately none recognized her and she could look around her shattered apartment at her leisure. Like most empty or abandoned houses in Aachen it had been looted by those who had remained in the city during the siege. She could find nothing of any use, save a few jars of preserves, which she found in the cellar, overlooked because the cellar entrance had been hidden by fallen masonry and beams.

She did not spend long in the apartment. She knew that in the evening there was a curfew for all Germans in the city. If she wanted to find out anything, she had to get on the streets now. Taking an old shopping basket she found lying amongst the rubble in the corner of the room, she went out into the street, looking like any suburban housewife going off shopping.

The first woman she asked told her all she wanted to know. The chief burgomaster was called Franz Oppenhoff and he lived in the Eupener Strasse. The middle-aged woman, who was wearing a pair of men's boots and clutching a loaf of bread under her arm as if her life depended upon it, asked Ilse if she knew where the street was.

Ilse nodded quickly. She did not want to arouse any suspicion that she was not from Aachen. 'Yes, on the way to the Belgian border, near Köpfchen.' Fortunately she could remember the name of the border-post.

'Yes, that's it,' the woman said.

'And the number?' Ilse asked just as a jeep filled with laughing, well-fed *Amis* passed. Quickly she averted her eyes.

'Number two hundred and fifty-one. One of those villas out there on the hill,' the woman answered. Ilse thanked her and walked on.

She was in a quandary. She felt like proceeding with the

mission in spite of the surprise encounter with the enemy soldier in the woods. But were the others still alive? And could she contact them if they were? She could not do the job by herself, since she had no weapon.

That afternoon she walked slowly out of the ruined town, past the tall, grey, three-storey bunkers, bearing the shell and bomb marks of last year's fighting, and began to climb the long hill which led to Köpfchen. Occasionally she met a woman or old man, bent double under a load of twigs and branches from the nearby forests, or dragging a wooden cart filled with potatoes. Once a truckload of American soldiers passed by and in spite of the penalties for fraternization with German women, several of them whistled at her. She looked the other way.

After walking for about three-quarters of an hour, she came to the crossroads where the Eupener Strasse started. She rested for a moment. To the casual observer she looked like any other female inhabitant of the captured city, taking advantage of the spring sunshine to do a little *hamstern*.[1] In fact, Ilse was scanning the area thoroughly, trying at the same time to see the dangers inherent in any action in that area and to understand the myriad military signs the *Amis* had posted at the cross-roads.

After a while she picked up her basket again and crossed to the right side of the Eupener Strasse, where the houses soon gave way to open fields, which at first she thought might provide her with an escape route. But her commonsense told her the nearer she got to the border, the more likely was it that there would be enemy troops in the vicinity.

The Eupener Strasse was a fairly steep road, bordered on one side by open fields and the tramline that in the old days had brought Belgian workers over the border to work in Aachen. Now the line was rusty and overgrown with grass. These days all the traffic was in the opposite direction. On the other side, large villas bordered the road, with intervals of up to fifty

[1] The process of finding food or fuel, called after a little animal which stuffs its cheeks with supplies.

metres between each house. Ilse noted, in particular, that most of the houses were protected from the curious eyes of people passing by on the road by tall hedges or rows of firs. Once anyone managed to penetrate the house, they would be able to do what they wanted, concealed from the road.

Then she came upon the house—Two hundred and fifty-one Eupener Strasse—the house where Franz Oppenhoff, the traitor, lived.

After a moment of indecision Ilse made up her mind. She walked across the cobbled street, avoiding the holes made by the shells, and opened the gate. The house was some two metres above street level and she had to climb six or seven steps to reach the door which was situated to the side of the house, fronted by a broad wooden-railed balcony running the length of the second storey. She made a mental note of the layout of the place.

Swiftly she ran her eye down the list of names written out carefully on a large sheet of paper nailed to the door (later she was to learn that the Americans had made the inhabitants of every house in the city do this). There was a couple of names she did not know, but those she sought were there: Oppenhoff Franz, Oppenhoff Irmgard and then three other names, Monika, Christa and Irmgard. She looked at the dates of birth behind each name. Monika would be eight, Christa seven and Irmgard still a baby—about eighteen months old. So the *Ami* traitor had children! The fact did not alter her determination to go on with the mission and she knocked on the door. For a moment nothing happened. Then there was a squeak of a door being opened to her left.

A pretty dark-haired woman of about her own age looked at her. '*Sie wunschen*?'[1] she queried.

Ilse licked her lips which had suddenly become very dry! 'I've been walking for a long time and I'm thirsty. I wonder if you could give me a glass of water?'

The woman, Oppenhoff's maid, Elisabeth Gillessen, smiled

[1] What can I do for you?

and smoothed her dark hair back from her pretty face. 'Of course', she said 'follow me'. Ilse walked down the steps and followed her into the dark cellar. 'The key to the front door has been lost,' the maid explained as she led the way 'and as we don't want to break the door down, we use the cellar.' She stopped. 'You know at night, you've got to lock up. Those *Amis* . . .' She left the sentence unfinished and Ilse smiled. Obviously the soldiers would be after such a pretty girl.

The two women emerged into a dark, tiled hall, the walls of which were decorated with eighteenth-century prints. From somewhere upstairs came the sound of children's laughter.

The maid clicked her tongue. 'Those children!' she exclaimed. 'They couldn't make more noise if they tried, could they?' Ilse nodded absently; her eyes were busy taking in the place. She saw that the only entrance from ground level was the cellar door. At night the windows would be covered with shutters or blackouts and they nearly all of them had their glass intact so that anyone breaking in would have to remove a pane. It seemed that the safest and quietest means of entry would be through the cellar.

The maid obviously thought that Ilse did not speak because she was too thirsty to do so. 'But let me go and get you a glass of water,' she said hastily and disappeared into another room.

It was at that moment that sixteen-year-old Christel Schütz entered the dark hall. She stopped when she saw the other woman standing there in the hall and then said automatically, '*Guten Tag*'.

'*Guten Tag*', Ilse replied. Then she started. She knew the girl! She did not remember her name, but she remembered that she had worked with her in the German Maiden group the previous year when they had been preparing little Christmas gifts for the men at the front. But the girl did not seem to recognize her. They chatted a moment or two about the fine spring weather and then the maid returned with a glass of water. Ilse drank it hastily, thankful that she did not have to continue the conversation.

Emptying the glass, she returned it to the maid and then after murmuring a few words of thanks, she picked up her basket and left, as she had come, through the cellar. Hurriedly she started to walk back down the hill into the city, anxious to get as far away as possible from the young girl who might suddenly remember her. She had not been walking for very long when, with a start she became aware of hurrying footsteps behind her. She felt her heart begin to thump and turning she saw the girl. She was smiling and obviously intent on catching up with her. Ilse stopped and waited for her to catch up.

'I know you, don't I'? she asked, before the girl could speak.

Christel Schütz stared at her. 'My name is Ilse Hirsch. Don't you remember how we worked together on the Christmas gifts?'

The light of recognition dawned on the other girl's face. 'Oh, yes, I remember now. You were . . .' she stopped short.

Ilse could read her mind. She was about to say, 'You were a group leader.' 'I've got no place to go for the night,' she said swiftly so that the other girl had no time to continue her train of thought. 'I've just come across the Rhine, but there's nothing left in my old flat.' While she spoke, Ilse's eyes watched the girl's face for a reaction. 'So I'm looking for a place where I can sleep for the night before I decide what to do next.'

Christel's innocent young face relaxed and Ilse realized, with relief, that she had swallowed the story. 'Why don't you come and spend the night at our place,' she said, and turning, she pointed back up the hill. 'I'm living up there at *Haus Pelikan*. We can put you up for one night if you like.'

Ilse put her arm round the girl and gave her a hug 'Oh, that is very kind of you. I'd love to.'

Two hours later, Ilse Hirsch, who had come to Aachen to murder a traitor, was busily occupied helping Christel to clean and dust a couple of rooms in *Haus Pelikan*, her normally deathly pale face flushed red with the exertion of washing windows and sweeping floors.

After Ilse had disappeared, the Werewolf group had reassembled in the wood and hidden in the undergrowth. Turning his head into the wind, Wenzel listened to ascertain whether they were still being followed[1] but there was no sound of any pursuit.

Morgenschweiss raised himself from the ground and pushing back his blond curls from his forehead said, 'I got him.' He touched the little Belgian pistol in his holster, 'I got him. Didn't you see?'

'Oh, shut you mouth,' Leitgeb said and breathed out hard. Looking at Wenzel, he snapped, 'What now?'

Wenzel licked his lips. 'Give me a chance, Sepp, give me a chance. The first thing we've got to establish is where we are. What do you think?' He looked across at Heidorn and Hennemann.

Heidorn coughed. He didn't know and he didn't care. He felt sick. After two nights in the forest and the shock of the encounter with the border guard, all he wanted to do was to crawl into bed, fall asleep and forget the whole business. He dropped his eyes; let the heroic Hennemann do the talking!

Hennemann was his usual slow self. Nothing seemed to shake him. He pouted thoughtfully and said slowly, 'I think we must be close to Aachen now. Probably somewhere to the north-west of the city.'

'Where?' Wenzel snapped.

'I don't know exactly, but I suggest we move off soon and then I should be able to spot a landmark.'

Wenzel nodded in agreement. 'Right then, let's get on.' He rose to his feet and slung his rucksack over his shoulder again. The others did the same except for Heidorn, who coughed hard and remained where he was lying.

'What's up with you?' Wenzel asked.

---

[1] Surprisingly enough, although Sgt Finders reported the 'saboteurs' to the nearest US unit, the Americans took no action save to send a patrol to collect the empty cartridge cases found at the spot where Josef Saive was shot.

'I don't feel so good,' Heidorn replied and coughed again.

Wenzel's hand fell to his pistol. 'Don't be a fool. We've got to get on.'

Reluctantly Heidorn got to his feet. If they ever got back from their impossible mission, he was sure he was going to have trouble with Wenzel. But all the same he realized that Wenzel was not a man to be fooled with. He slung his rucksack and stumbled after the others through the wood.

They walked for several hours until they spotted the well-known Aachen landmark the *Dreilanderblick*.[1] Surprisingly enough it was Heidorn who saw it first. '*Dreilanderblick*,' he said weakly to Hennemann.

The group stopped at once while Hennemann followed the direction of Heidorn's outstretched hand. 'Yes,' he confirmed 'you're right.' After walking a little further, they flopped down into an exhausted sleep despite the damp cold of the forest, resting till the early hours of the morning. They then set off again, Hennemann in the lead. Now that he knew where they were, he guided them swiftly and efficiently through the dense woods which surround Aachen. Before the war he had served as a border policeman at the little border station of Köpfchen, not far from the Oppenhoff house, and he decided to take the Werewolf team across the border once more into Belgian territory where they could set up a base camp near his old station.

Thus it was that at the same time as Ilse Hirsch returned to her old apartment, preparatory to setting out to find the burgomaster, the five Werewolf men slipped across the Eupener Strasse, only five hundred metres from his house, and disappeared unobserved into the Belgian forest.

On the morning of the 22nd, they set up camp in the *Aachener Wald* (the Aachen Forest) just outside of town and began to plan their next move. For a while they could not come to any decision. Ilse's disappearance had upset their plans. Who would carry out the scout mission within the city itself? In

[1] The three country lookout, a hill feature from which the viewer can look out over three frontiers.

the end Wenzel decided that Sepp would sneak into town with Morgenschweiss. The two of them were to find out the general situation, the name and address of the chief burgomaster, and if they could—Ilse Hirsch.

When Wenzel had finished his briefing, Heidorn raised himself up from the blankets. His face was flushed with fever and his eyes glazed. 'Sepp, if you get a chance have a look at my old apartment in the Bismarck Strasse. Perhaps you . . .'

'Shut up!' Wenzel cut him off. 'Sepp has more important things to do than look for your flat, you fool.'

Heidorn let his head flop back on the blanket and kept silent.

Wenzel gave the two who were to go into town a quick scrutiny. 'Yes, you look all right. Erich,' he nodded to Morgenschweiss, 'knock that dirt off your pants. You don't want to give away the fact that you have been sleeping rough. The *Amis* aren't blind, you know!' Hurriedly Morgenschweiss did as he was told, then with a brief handshake, he and Leitgeb disappeared into the trees and were gone.

Ilse was glad to get away from Christel's. The girl was beginning to ask too many questions. She had tried to escape from her eager curiosity by going out for the rest of the day but in the evening she had to return because of the curfew; she did not want to be picked up by the *Ami* patrols without a pass. Before they went to bed, the girl had again pestered her with questions, particularly about what was going on on the German side of the line. She knew that sooner or later the girl would ask her directly what she was doing in Aachen.

In the end she accepted a dress from the girl (she had explained she had lost all her clothes in the siege of Aachen), and with the advice that she should get herself a pass as soon as possible, she left the apartment.

It was now over forty-eight hours since she had been separated from the group. During that period she had found out exactly who their intended victim was as well as the place where he lived. But at the same time she had discovered the true state of

126

the war from her conversations with Christel (though naturally she was not prepared to accept the girl's version of Germany's situation completely). All the same, discounting the effect of *Ami* propaganda on the naive sixteen-year-old, she realized that the end of the Third Reich was close at hand. Cologne, Bonn, Koblenz—all the major cities west of the Rhine—had fallen, and now the enemy was preparing to cross the Rhine itself.[1] Soon, it was obvious, Germany would have to surrender.

In the light of this situation, what should she do? In the end, after persistent questioning by Christel, she had told her that she had to make her way back to her Cologne headquarters. Christel had countered that Cologne had already fallen to the Americans—so why risk her life trying to get through the enemy lines.

Ilse had nodded thoughtfully as she had listened to the girl's advice and then asked how she should set about attempting to stay in the city. What were the formalities?

Christel had replied she would have to go to the pass office in the Suermondt Museum where the *Amis* had their headquarters; she would get her residence pass there, which she needed not only for the *Ami* MPs but also in order to obtain a ration card.

Later when she was interrogated by the British security officers Ilse maintained that she had not abandoned the project to murder the burgomaster because she was afraid for her life—'there had been a lot of talk before the operation of liquidating any traitor among us.' But after she had been separated from the others for two days, she had decided to apply for a pass, look for work in Aachen and forget the whole thing on the assumption that they had already been arrested.[2]

She was walking past the old Labour Exchange in the Auguststrasse when she heard an urgent whisper behind her, 'Ilse!' She spun round quickly at the mention of her name, her

---

[1] Montgomery's major assault on the Rhine began, in fact, that same evening.

[2] Naturally it is impossible to check the truth of this to-day. However it must be pointed out that if Ilse Hirsch thought the rest had already been arrested, then she must have expected to be arrested herself. Why, then, didn't she escape while she was able to do so?

heart in her mouth. It was Morgenschweiss. His parachutist's coverall was gone now and although he was still wearing his oversized American rubber boots, he looked like any other youngster to be seen that day on the streets of the occupied city. Behind him some twenty metres off, lounging against a bullet-pocked wall, looking as if he had nothing to do with Morgenschweiss, Leitgeb was positioned, one hand dug deep in his pocket. Ilse knew that the Austrian NCO's hand was tightly clenched around the butt of his pistol. He was covering the boy.

'Mensch, Ilse!' Morgenschweiss exclaimed, 'we thought you were arrested or dead!'

'I thought the same about you,' Ilse cried, shaking Morgenschweiss' hand. 'But where are you?'

Morgenschweiss looked up and down the street carefully, as if he were afraid anyone could overhear, though there was no one within listening distance. 'Up in the woods near Köpfchen.'

'*Köpfchen*,' Ilse echoed, 'that's where he is—the burgomaster.' Morgenschweiss nodded. 'Later, let's get back to the camp.' He and the girl went up to Leitgeb. 'Sepp,' he said, 'we're going back. I'll go first, then, Ilse, you come after me, keeping your distance. Sepp can bring up the rear. Understand?

'Yes,' Ilse answered, almost in a daze. The operation was on again. There'd be no staying in Aachen now and looking for work.

IV

Franz Oppenhoff was tired—very tired. The constant conflict with the Americans, the dangers presented by the Ardennes Offensive, the long winter and the lack of food had all taken their toll. When his wife and children had at last dared to return to the city in February, Irmgard Oppenhoff was shocked by the change in her husband's appearance during the six months he had been chief burgomaster. His ruddy, healthy look had vanished. Now, his face was pale and there were dark bags under his eyes. It was obvious that he was not only under-nourished but also under severe mental strain.

In the old days her husband had been a jolly man, a typical Rhinelander who had enjoyed loud, lively conversation and was never at a loss for words. Now he was given to moods of despair and he would sink into long silences, from which he could not be roused even by the children. He was continually making macabre references to the 'bullet which has already been made for me', as if he reckoned daily with an attempt on his life, although his wife and friends constantly reassured him that the war was almost finished and with it the danger to his life. But Franz Oppenhoff could not be convinced. 'I know their Gestapo methods,' he told his wife more than once, 'they'll get me in the end. Somewhere or other there is already one of their para-troopers assigned to the job of murdering me.'

Irmgard Oppenhoff was worried, but she did not let her husband see her anxiety. Instead, being a practical, realistic person, she decided to do as much as she could to calm her husband. Now that the winter was over and the sun was beginning to shine, she felt that she could shake her husband out of his depression, 'Why,' she told him, 'next year at this time we'll be celebrating Carnival again. You wait and see!'

Thus it was that she planned to make the Palm Sunday week-end of March, 1945, a special one for her husband. For the first time since she had come back to Aachen, they would have the house to themselves, since the couple billeted with them would be elsewhere in the city over the weekend. On Saturday morning she sent her husband off to 'organize'—the euphemism they all used for black market purchases—sugar and coal. Her husband was like a child when it came to sweet things and she wanted to give him a treat. That evening they were to remain alone at home and the following evening they were invited to Dr Faust's house a little way down the Eupener Strasse. Faust had 'organized' some schnapps from the one brewery which had been re-opened and was giving a modest little party.

All in all Irmgard felt that the weekend would rouse her husband out of his depression and drive the ever-present preoccupation with death out of his mind. She was determined to make a success of the two days at her disposal.

In the early hours of Saturday morning, the Werewolf team moved to its last camp, crossing the Eupener Strasse once more and taking up a position in the woods near the small Belgian village of Hauset, some ninety minutes on foot from Oppenhoff's house. As Hennemann had anticipated, they met no one and they reached their destination without incident, save that again Heidorn was proving a nuisance. All during the march he kept urging Hennemann to 'keep out' of the planned murder. 'I don't want you to go with them,' he told the other guide, 'I'm going to Aachen anyway, whatever you do. I want nothing to do with the whole dirty business.' Hennemann had ignored him and had concentrated on finding the way through the trees.

Palm Sunday dawned a fine bright spring day. The men rose stiffly and disappeared into the bushes to complete their morning toilet while Ilse opened her last jar of preserved fruit. Wenzel had forbidden them to light a fire in case they gave their position away.

Everything now was planned. The boy, Ilse and Heidorn would remain in the camp while Wenzel and Leitgeb would carry out the mission, guided by Hennemann. Thanks to Ilse, they now knew the only danger to their plan was the presence of an *Ami* general's HQ close to the traitor's house. But with a laugh Wenzel had assured them that the *Amis* would be either drunk or asleep when they struck, for he planned to carry out the 'job' near midnight when they were very unlikely to meet anybody except their intended victim.

The day passed slowly. Everyone was tense, yet no one spoke any further about their mission, except when Wenzel remarked briefly that, if anything happened, the group which remained behind should make its own way (under Heidorn's guidance) back to the Werewolf headquarters in Hülchrath. Hennemann rejoined by remarking to Heidorn that if they were forced to break up, they would meet again at one of two hunting lodges they both knew in the woods near the Belgian border village of Elsenborn or further inland near the German village of Reinartzhof.

Heidorn, who was feeling sick, nodded miserably and again told Hennemann not to participate in the actual murder, and again Hennemann refused to answer him. Giving up his old comrade completely, the younger guide rolled over in his blankets and went to sleep.

Afternoon came and high overhead the conspirators heard the drone of heavy planes. It went on for hours and once or twice Morgenschweiss was tempted to go out into the open to have a look at the enemy planes flying eastwards, but Wenzel told him to keep under cover.[1] In the forest it grew warm. Ilse stretched out in a patch of sunlight and felt its rays penetrate the thin material of her borrowed dress. Heidorn snored and Wenzel and Leitgeb napped a little way off. Only Hennemann was still on his feet walking nervously round the limited area of their camp. In a few hours, as soon as darkness fell, they would be off.

In the Eupener Strasse the Sunday passed pleasantly for the Oppenhoff family. In the morning they went to church to listen to the Palm Sunday mass and afterwards Irmgard Oppenhoff gave her husband a good meal of onions and potatoes followed by 'real bean coffee', with three spoons of sugar as a special treat.

In the afternoon they prepared their garden for the first vegetables of the year. In the old days before the war they would never have dared work outside in public on Sunday, but now there were no curious neighbours to bother them anymore. Sometimes Irmgard would cycle half-an-hour into the city to see her husband in his office and never meet a soul. Apart from the few occupied houses about them, the suburb was a deserted ruin. Carefully they raked the ground clear of rubble and pebbles, listening now and again to the noise made

[1] The planes were the follow-up for Montgomery's crossing of the Rhine.

10. *The meadow where Leitgeb, Wenzel and Henneman spent the night of 25 March.*

11. *The Oppenhoff house today.*

12. *Chief Burgomaster Franz Oppenhoff.*

by their three children at the back of the house; then, satisfied with their work, they began to plant the precious beans which they hoped would provide them with a source of food in the autumn. As they worked the sun beat down warmly on their backs. Husband and wife were happy to be together, away from the war and its problems for a few hours at least.

At six o'clock they gave the children a single slice of bread each, covered with *Sirop*, a synthetic treacle which at least tasted sweet and staved off the children's almost continual pangs of hunger, and packed them off to bed on the undamaged upper floor. But Monika would not go off to sleep straight away and Franz had to go upstairs once more and give the eight-year-old girl another good-night kiss.

Finally the children were quiet. The burgomaster put on his jacket and the armband indicating his office round his right arm in case they came home after the curfew and were stopped by an American patrol. Giving the maid her instructions, he took a final glance at the three sleeping children and followed his wife out through the cellar door.

V

They left the Hauset camp for the last time just as the sun started to set. Shaking hands with the other two (Heidorn buried his head in his blankets and pretended to be asleep), they threw their bread bags[1] over their shoulders and set off. Hennemann took the lead, with Sepp in the middle and Wenzel some twenty metres to the rear.

Swiftly they made their way through the wood, crossed the Belgian–German frontier and headed for the Eupener Strasse. It was a fine moonlit night and Hennemann, who knew the road like the back of his hand, made good time, so that they

[1] A bread bag was standard German Army equipment, being a small canvas bag in which the soldier carried his daily bread ration.

arrived at their destination shortly after nine. Wenzel now took charge. He signalled to them to follow him into a nearby field, some hundred and fifty metres away from the Oppenhoff house. 'You stay here,' he told Hennemann, 'and look after our gear.' He unslung his bread bag and dropped it with a few other odds and ends in the field. Sepp followed suit. A few moments later they were gone, leaving a somewhat nervous Hennemann standing there alone, his pistol drawn, as if he expected an *Ami* patrol to appear out of the trees at any minute.

Leitgeb cut through the telephone wire with his wire cutters. 'All right,' he whispered softly, 'They can't contact anybody now.'

Silently in their rubber-soled boots, they sneaked across the garden which separated them from the Oppenhoff house. At once Wenzel found the cellar door that Ilse had told him about. It was locked. Noiselessly he released the door handle and looked at the window nearby. It was small, but both he and Sepp were slim enough to get through. 'The window,' he whispered.

The other man nodded.

Wenzel applied pressure. With a loud click the catch gave. The window swung up to reveal nothing but blackness. Wenzel felt his heart beating rapidly. He turned his head to one side. Not a sound. Nobody had heard them. Nothing but the faint sound of the wind in the tops of the trees.

Swiftly he crawled through the open window and dropped down on the other side. Sepp followed him, then closed the window behind them. The SS officer switched on his flashlight and shone it around the cellar. The beam picked up a pile of empty bottles, a carefully stacked heap of coal, a wheelless cycle—the usual contents of a cellar. Then he spotted the stairs leading up into the house. 'Over here,' he said.

Cautiously they climbed the stone cellar steps and found themselves in a small hallway. There was still no sound save the ticking of a clock somewhere in the darkness. 'Are they all in bed?' Sepp asked.

'I don't know,' Wenzel whispered, 'but we'll soon find out.'

He set his foot carefully on the first step of the wooden staircase leading to the next floor where presumably the bedrooms were. It squeaked alarmingly and Wenzel gave a jump. Anxiously he waited for a shout of alarm to come from above but everything remained silent.

Treading as lightly as he could and keeping to the side of the steps where the staircase seemed more solid, he began a slow ascent, followed by Sepp who held his cocked pistol at the ready. They came to the first door. Moving very deliberately Wenzel nodded to the Austrian to get ready, then pressing his body against the wall, he reached out and slowly opened the door. Sepp flashed his blue light inside.

'Kids,' he whispered.

Wenzel looked over his shoulder. Three children lay curled up beneath the heavy German goosefeather-filled quilts. 'His,' he said and, very quietly, he closed the door and on the tips of their toes they moved on to the next door. The room was empty as was the next. No one save the children seemed to be in the house. Where was Oppenhoff? Had Ilse lied? Had they come all this way to be cheated of their victim? Had the *Amis* . . .

Wenzel's train of thought was broken by Leitgeb's urgent whisper. 'Listen! There's somebody in there!'

Wenzel was sweating heavily. With his free hand he wiped his brow and listened. Sepp was right. There was somebody on the other side of the door. The heavy regular breathing of someone asleep was distinct enough. Pressing himself hard against the wall, he nodded to Leitgeb. The Austrian took up the same position as before, his torch ready and pistol pointing directly at the door. Steeling himself for the scream that might come at any instant, Wenzel pushed the door. It gave with a creak. He felt his heart jump.

'Who's there?'

The voice was feminine, young and scared.

Wenzel pushed himself in front of Leitgeb. A young woman

with dark hair and pale scared face was sitting up in bed, the clothes clutched to her chest in the classic pose of female fear.

He licked his dry lips. 'Where's the Burgomaster—Burgomaster Oppenhoff?' he asked thickly, hardly recognizing his own voice. He could barely keep it under control.

Elisabeth Gillenssen was frightened out of her wits. Ever since she had first got to know the *Amis* when they had captured Eupen in September, she had been pestered by their advances. There weren't many pretty girls around and the sex-starved GIs were always trying to get her into bed with their broken German and standard offer '*Du schlafen mit me, baby, ich bringen du chocolate.*' Now one of them had broken into the house while the Oppenhoffs were absent. Who else but an *Ami* would be about at this time of night?

But the strange man repeated his question. 'I asked where the Burgomaster is?'

'He's not here,' she stammered.

'Where is he then?'

'Next door at our neighbours—at the Faust house.'

'Then get up and fetch him,' the man in the door said.

'But I've got to get dressed to do that,' she protested, shielding her eyes against the blue light and trying to identify the two strangers at the door. All she could make out was a sort of uniform jacket without any badges and what looked to her like American khaki trousers.[1]

Wenzel turned to Leitgeb. 'Turn off the torch,' he commanded. Then to the girl. 'Get dressed. We'll wait for you downstairs.' Swiftly the 21-year-old maid got dressed and hurried downstairs, feeling her way with the aid of matches (Aachen was still without electric light). There was no sign of the two strangers. But she did notice that in the ground floor all the doors were

[1] In fact, the two killers were wearing German Air Force parachute coveralls with civilian clothes underneath. In case they were captured they did not want to be shot as spies, and the Hague Land Warfare Convention stated that if at least one piece of military clothing were worn the prisoner in question must be treated as a POW.

wide-open, as if the two men had searched the house till they had found her.

Overcome by fear, she ran to the toilet and locking herself in, opened the window that looked out to the little meadow above the house. For a moment she could not see anything. Then, helped by the moon which slid suddenly from behind a cloud, she saw three men, two standing out in the open, and another positioned under a tree. She could see the men in the open quite clearly. One was bigger and broader than the other and she noted that his features had a strong Slavic cast. It was Wenzel.

'What do you want now?' she called, controlling herself, feeling a little safer since the door was locked behind her.

'We want a pass,' one of them replied, coming a little closer to the window.

'Why would an American want a pass?' she called, still thinking they were *Amis*.

'Don't ask too many questions, girl,' the stranger ordered, 'go and get Oppenhoff.'

At that moment the other man stepped into the moonlight which now flooded the little meadow and she could distinctly see him playing with a pistol. Leitgeb threw it up into the air, caught it and twirled it around his finger. Up, down, around. It was like the cowboys she remembered from the American *Wildwest-filme* from before the war. Elisabeth did not need to be told again. She opened the toilet door and ran into the dining room. There she crawled through the window and hurried over to the Faust house where the party was still in progress. Even before she opened the door to the room in which they were sitting, nursing their precious schnapps by the light of a solitary candle, she was crying 'Herr Oppenhoff . . . Herr Oppenhoff . . . there are American soldiers . . . they want to speak to you . . . Now!'

Franz Oppenhoff rose with a start. American soldiers! What did they want from him at this time of night? Had something gone wrong in the town? For a moment he was undecided

Why did he have to go over to them? Couldn't they come over here and speak to him? But then he decided that if he asked the maid to bring them over, they might see the precious schnapps and ask for a drink. He knew his GIs. And there wasn't really enough to go round even for the present company. 'All right, Elisabeth,' he said, 'I'm coming.'

Pulling on his gloves and straightening his armband, he turned to Faust, 'you speak English, Faust. You'd better come with me.' Faust rose to his feet and together the two men went outside to where the maid was waiting. Oppenhoff gave her the key to the cellar door. 'You open it,' he said. 'Now where are they?'

The maid did not need to answer his question. The three strangers stepped into the path and asked directly, 'Are you the Burgomaster of Aachen?' They spoke German.

Faust said in English, 'What do you want?'

The first stranger, it was Wenzel, replied in German, 'We're not *Amis*. We're German airmen. We were shot down near Brussels three days ago. Now we're trying to make our way back to the German lines. What about getting us passes, Herr Bürgermeister?'

Standing there in the moonlight while Elisabeth fumbled with the cellar door a few yards away, Oppenhoff shook his head. 'I can't do that. You should report to the Americans and give yourselves up. The war's nearly over anyway. It's only a matter of days.'

Abruptly Leitgeb snapped, 'Heil Hitler.'

Faust, standing next to Oppenhoff, started. It was a long time now since he had heard that greeting. Somehow at this time of night and in this place, it frightened him. He stared warily at the three men, while Oppenhoff continued talking, noting that one had a pistol stuck in his pocket. It was a German Walther pistol. He recognized it from his days as a trial engineer in the small arms section the Rheinmetall armaments factory. He noted too that none of the three wore badges of rank on their uniform jackets and all three were bare-headed. Fear overcame him suddenly and he knew that something terrible was going to happen. He had to get help.

Oppenhoff was just saying, 'Let me get you something to eat,' when Faust cut in, 'I'll go back to my house and see what I can find there for you.' And with that he was gone, walking back as hurriedly as he dared without arousing the suspicions of the three strangers.

At last the maid got the door of the cellar open. 'Don't be alarmed, Elisabeth', Oppenhoff attempted to calm her. 'They're German fliers. Make them a couple of sandwiches if you can find something.' Then turning to the two men—Hennemann had moved away—he said, 'Just a minute, I'll help her.' He followed her down the cellar stairs into the darkness.

When he was gone, Leitgeb hissed urgently to Wenzel. 'When he comes up again!'

In the light of the moon, Wenzel's face suddenly went pale, the cold silver rays giving it a strange green hue. 'Yes, now,' he replied hoarsely.

Almost hesitantly he drew the pistol with its long silencer. Leitgeb saw to his alarm that the officer's hand trembled as he did so. 'Be quick,' he urged. 'The other one's gone off to alarm the *Amis*. Believe me, Wenzel!'

There were sounds from below. It was Oppenhoff coming back. As Elisabeth, busy cutting the brown heavy loaf she had taken from the stone jar in the kitchen, turned to watch him go, she caught a last glance of him digging his hands deeply into his jacket pockets. It was a characteristic gesture and she had been long enough with Oppenhoff to know that it meant he was very nervous.

The footsteps were getting closer. Leitgeb and Wenzel crouched close to the cellar door. Leitgeb could hear Wenzel's rapid shallow breathing. Suddenly the traitor appeared in front of them—*but Wenzel did not fire*.

'Do it!' Leitgeb hissed.

Wenzel did not reply.

'You cowardly sow!' the Austrian cried and snatched the pistol from him.

'What?' Oppenhoff opened his mouth to protest, but it was too late.

Swiftly Leitgeb thrust the pistol at Oppenhoff's head. Now he knew Wenzel for what he was. In spite of the secrecy, the posturing, the different uniforms, the tales of his days with Skorzeny and all the rest of it, the SS officer was a filthy coward after all. In a fury, he levelled the pistol directly at the burgomaster's left temple. An instant's hesitation and then he fired.

Up in the kitchen, still cutting the heavy hard bread, Elisabeth Gillessen heard a sound which she later described as being 'like an unoiled door creaking.' For a moment she paused in her task, then thinking no more of the unusual sound, she continued cutting.

Faust returned to the company, his face pale. Before he spoke, he lit a cigarette by means of the solitary candle. Sitting opposite him at the table Irmgard Oppenhoff could see how his hand trembled and tiny drops of wax fell on the tablecloth. Breathing out a thin stream of blue smoke, he said, 'No need to worry.' He looked at Frau Oppenhoff. 'All routine.'

'Who is it?' she asked.

'German fliers. They crashed or were shot down near Brussels. They are trying to make their way back to their own lines. Now they need passes and food. Your husband is making them a few sandwiches.'

Irmgard Oppenhoff's eyes grew round with fear. As she was to state later, 'the news went through me like an electrical shock.' 'We can't leave my husband alone with them,' she cried, jumping to her feet. 'For heaven's sake, if they are Germans and my husband gives them anything to eat, it might cost him his life.'

Later she could never decide whether she meant the Americans might execute him for aiding escaped German soldiers or whether she thought the strangers were the executioners that her husband was always talking about.

She looked at Dr Op de Hit, an old acquaintance of her husband's, 'Will you come with me?'

Hastily he rose to his feet, 'Yes, come on.' Together they ran out into the open.

'There's someone coming,' Wenzel whispered, rousing himself from the trance he had been in since Leitgeb had seized the pistol from him. 'Let's go.'

Leitgeb grabbed him. 'Wait a minute, you pig!' he called angrily. 'We've got to have proof.' He bent down to where Oppenhoff lay dead on the cellar steps, the bullet hole clearly visible in his temple. Swiftly he tugged the armband from his sleeve and pulled off his gloves.

Suddenly there was a volley of shots.

'*Amis!*' Leitgeb yelled.

A patrol from a nearby Signal Corps unit was out looking for the break in the line, where Leitgeb had snipped through the wires. They had spotted Hennemann crouched in the shadow of a tree and opened fire at once. With all his strength Hennemann pelted across the fields. Behind him he could hear shots and white tracer began to rip through the night. At last he reached the shelter of a tree-lined side street. He sprinted across the Eupener Strasse and into the fields on the other side. Suddenly he became aware of someone running behind him. He drew his pistol. The dark figure came closer. The man was alone. Hennemann's finger curled around the trigger. Then he saw that it was Wenzel. He was gasping for breath and there were beads of sweat running down his pale face.

'Where's Sepp?'

'On the other side of the road . . . he's all right . . . Come on, let's get out of here . . . Come on.' Together they started to run again.

Irmgard Oppenhoff's hand flew to her mouth and stifled the cry when she saw her husband lying crumpled on the steps. Then she stumbled back against Doctor Op de Hit. '*Der Franz . . . Franz ist tot!*'[1] Operation Carnival was over.

[1] Franz is dead.

V

The Last Battle

'Je stärker der Sturm, desto kräftiger der Widerstand.'[1]

Dr Goebbels, Nazi Propaganda Minister, April, 1945

[1] 'The stronger the storm, the mightier the resistance.'

I

The news that the first Allied-appointed burgomaster of an occupied German city had been murdered was flashed round the world. The *New York Times* headlined the story as 'Non-Nazi Mayor of Aachen Killed by 3 German Chutists in Uniform,' and commented, 'The assassins shot the Mayor in gangster fashion and escaped. Hitler often has threatened retaliation against Germans who co-operated.'

The London *Times* was more reserved and simply ran the Reuter report that 'Oppenhoff, who was 41, was an attorney and had been burgomaster for 8 months. He was a right wing Catholic, but had never been active in opposing the Nazis. He was chosen by the Allied authorities because of his administrative experience and the authority he enjoyed in Catholic circles.' All the same the newspaper registered shock at the fact that such things could still happen in occupied Germany and reported that the 'patrol on duty in the street chased the three men and fired at them but was unable to catch them.'

The news of Oppenhoff's death brought a feeling of despair to the Allied headquarters in France and Luxemburg, especially when, in the last days of March, Goebbels' propaganda machine went into action and revealed what organization had committed the murder. The feeling aroused by the murder was to have a decisive effect on allied strategy for the rest of the war in Europe.

On 29 March Goebbels' German Press Agency announced boldly that 'The Burgomaster of Aachen, the lawyer Franz Oppenhoff' had been executed at the orders of the 'German People's Court of Justice' because of 'collaboration with the enemy.'

This bold announcement, which was based on Allied reports, because as yet Berlin still had no word directly from the murderers who were now fleeing through the Eifel, was taken up immediately by the Nazi press. The *Flensburger Nachrichten* for 31 March wrote, 'As reported by the official English news agency, Reuter, and confirmed by Allied military authorities, the Allied-appointed burgomaster of Aachen, Franz Oppenhoff was killed a few days ago by German freedom-fighters.[1] We would like to add this information to the news. Oppenhoff was condemned to death by the "Court for the Preservation of German Honour" immediately he entered the service of the hated enemy.' The Berlin *Völkischer Beobachter* took up the same theme, commenting, 'A dishonourable treacherous creature deserved the fate he brought upon himself by his actions. And in the future anyone who infringes the highest law of the land, the law of national honour and loyalty, will inevitably meet the same fate.'

In the last days of March and the first weeks of April, the press was full of tales, true and imagined, calculated to alarm Allied Intelligence at the prospect of fighting a protracted partisan war with the Germans once the real fighting was over, and to bolster up the German will to resist in the last great battle.

On 1 April, the shock caused in the Allied camp by the Oppenhoff murder was heightened by the first broadcast of a new German radio station—*Radio Werwolf*.

Radio Werwolf had nothing to do with the Himmler organization, but the Allied intelligence officers and monitors busily recording its first broadcast were not to know that. For the first time they now knew the name of the organization which had murdered Oppenhoff, and for those of them who knew their German history the name aroused memories of the traditional German *Femegerichte*[2] which dated back to the Middle Ages.

During the decline of the Holy Roman Empire groups of disgruntled knights formed vigilante societies which met in secret to pass sentence of death on those whom they felt were contributing to the increasing anarchy in Germany. At trials which had no legal foundation they swore on pain of death

---

[1] It is interesting to note that the designation so beloved by to-day's urban guerrillas was already in use a quarter of a century ago.

[2] Roughly, 'court of revenge'.

'to hold and conceal the Holy Veme from wife and child, from father and mother, from sister and brother, from fire and wind, from everything upon which the sun shines or the rain falls, from everything between earth and heaven.'

The trials were conducted with elaborate rituals and the accused, if he were present and found guilty, would be hanged and buried in the middle of the night; if the guilty person were not present, however, he would be then deemed *Vogelfrei*[1] which meant that any member of the court could kill him without penalty.

These secret tribunals have occurred throughout German history. In particular, after the First World War ex-officers took vengeance on the 'November criminals', as they called those politicians who had negotiated with the Allies in November, 1918, and brought about the shameful *Versaillesdiktat*. Two leading liberal politicians were murdered by the execution squads. *Radio Werwolf* and Goebbels' vitriolic speeches seemed to indicate that the whole vicious business was to begin again.

In those last weeks of the war Josef Goebels was in his element. At last the born demagogue who hated the world because it had made him under-sized and deformed could give free rein to his hatred. Nor did it matter if that hatred was not only directed at the enemy but also at his own people who had failed him in his megalomaniac designs. His countrymen had to be shaken out of their petty-bourgeois *gemütlich* complacency and made to realize that if Germany fell, then they too must fall with it.

Radio Werwolf was an ideal instrument for his hatred. Time and again it hammered out the twin message '*destroy the enemy or destroy yourself*! Civilian or soldier, whether you are still unoccupied or deep behind the enemy lines, fight on!'

'There is no end to revolution,' cried *Radio Werwolf*. 'A revolution is only doomed to failure if those who make it cease to be revolutionaries. Together with the monuments of culture there crumble also the last obstacles to the fulfilment

[1] Literally 'bird-free', i.e. to be dealt with like a gamebird.

of our revolutionary task. Now that everything is in ruins, we are forced to rebuild Europe. In the past, private possessions tied us to a bourgeois restraint. Now the bombs, instead of killing all Europeans, have only smashed the prison walls which held them captive. In trying to destroy Europe's future, the enemy has only succeeded in smashing its past; and with that, everything old and outworn has gone.'

It was the true nihilistic voice of the Nazi creed—the only authentic voice of Nazism, whose leaders generally had been softened and inhibited by the years of power. Although Goebbels' preaching had very little to do with the real aims of Himmler's organization, he was believed by both Allied intelligence and the German people. In particular, the young men and women, who had not yet witnessed the realities of the front, but who had been schooled from their earliest years in the self-sacrificing philosophies of the Nazi youth organizations, now came flocking to Himmler's flag to serve in the new organization, prepared to fight to the last, fired by the spate of new slogans Goebbels had launched over his propaganda station—'Rather dead than red!'. . . 'People to Arms!'. . . 'We will win all the same!' and the most popular one of all—'The stronger the storm, the mightier the resistance!'

Himmler did not approve of the opening of Goebbels' *Radio Werwolf*, with its persistent message hammered home every hour that 'we will fight on even if we suffer military defeat'. In his opinion, the German people should not be allowed to believe that the Army might fail to stop the Allied attack. Only a few days before General Gehlen, of the German intelligence,[1] who had long studied the organization of the Polish

[1] The mysterious Gehlen, who did not allow himself to be photographed for 20 years after the war, took off with his whole organization after the war and offered its invaluable knowledge of the Russians to the Americans. The CIA accepted and Gehlen began work with his former enemies almost immediately. A few years later the 'Gehlen Organization' became the nucleus of the German Secret Service. In 1971 ex-General Gehlen created a world sensation when he revealed that the 'Brown Eminence', Martin Borman, the man behind Hitler had been a Soviet spy all along.

13. *Heidorn after his arrest.*   14. *Frau Dr Oehlert.*

15. *Henneman, Heidorn and Hirsch at their trial.*

16. *Three brothers, aged between ten and fourteen, who were caught sniping at American troops in Aachen. They are typical of the kind of resistance encouraged by the Werewolves.*

17. *Secret photograph of SS General Gutenberger, taken in Werl Military Prison in 1946, when he was serving 12 years for war crimes.*

resistance movement had forwarded him a carefully drawn up plan for a German movement on the same lines.

Himmler's reaction made Major-General Schellenberg, the SS secret service officer who presented the plan to his boss, tremble for his life.

'This is complete madness,' the Reichsführer cried. 'If I were to discuss such a plan with Wench,[1] I should be denounced as the first defeatist in the Third Reich. The fact would be served up to the Fuehrer piping hot!' And he went on to denounce 'high-class staff officers' who sat safely behind the lines nursing plans for the post-war period instead of going to the front like himself and getting on with the fighting.

As he envisaged the Werewolves, they were to be a para-military organization which would never operate after defeat, but would be solely an auxiliary formation that might carry the war behind the Allied lines as a diversionary movement. But in order to do this, the Werewolves would have to remain a secret organization. Now, however, Goebbels had made the new guerrilla formation known to a wide public, and he had to do something to accommodate the flood of eager young volunteers who were coming forward.

Pruetzmann, the nominal head of the organization, was ordered to set up training schools for the volunteers and comb the Berlin ministries for suitable female instructors to staff these schools (the SS provided the male instructors). Pruetzmann set about the task without any enthusiasm. His personality had changed a great deal since the previous November when he had first been given command of the Werewolves. His vanity had vanished. He knew the war was over for Germany. She had lost and he would soon have to account for his crimes in the East. Now his mood wavered between moments of confidence in which he felt he might yet save his skin by 'going underground' (as so many of his SS and Gestapo colleagues were planning to do) or desperate drunken hours when he realized there was only one way out for him—suicide.

[1] CO of the 12th German Army fighting on the Elbe.

But if Pruetzmann no longer cared about the organization he commanded, his subordinates, enthusiastic young SS officers and female officials of the youth organizations and the *Arbeits-dienst*,[1] certainly did. They believed in his organization which, according to Himmler, was 'born of the National Socialist spirit'. Schools were set up everywhere in which the students were trained to sabotage enemy transport and communications by cutting tyres or pouring sugar in petrol tanks. But the instruction did not stop at sabotage. The students were also taught how to kill by poisoning wells and food supplies and some groups were even equipped with large quantities of arsenic specifically for this purpose. For, as Himmler himself declared that spring, 'Every Bolshevik, every Briton, every American found on German soil is our legitimate prey. In such cases, our movement does not need to take into account the conventions observed by the regular armed forces.' And these trainee murderers were not to confine their attentions to the enemy but to kill any German who collaborated with him. From Pruetzmann's office the order went out, 'Every burgomaster in Allied-held territory is to be liquidated at the earliest possible opportunity.'[2]

In the main these training schools were situated in the suburbs of Berlin or in the surrounding country districts, but as the Russians got closer to the capital, it was clear that schools had to be opened further afield. It was decided, therefore, to send an SS Colonel named Siebl to Austria to open schools there. Siebl opened his first Werewolf training school in the middle of an area which Allied intelligence was already beginning to call the 'Alpine Fortress' or 'Redoubt'. It was a fortuitous choice but soon created great alarm amongst the Allies.

[1] The labour service in which every German boy and girl had to serve for six months usually in their eighteenth year.

[2] It is ironic to note in this context that Lt-Col Neinhaus's own brother, Dr Neinhaus, Mayor of Heidelberg, was threatened with murder because he had surrendered the city without a fight. One wonders if one of the men or women trained by his brother at Hülchrath was scheduled to do the job.

II

The American press had first started worrying about a last-ditch stand of die-hard Nazis back in December, 1944. On the 15th of that month the military expert of the New York communist *Daily Worker* had predicted that Hitler would never surrender but would flee to the Alpine region of Bavaria and Austria and make a last-ditch stand with his élite SS and mountain troops.

During the Battle of the Bulge the 'Alpine Redoubt' was not forgotten by Goebbels. At a secret meeting of all German editors and leading journalists in December, he told them they must never mention the 'Redoubt' and if they read reports of it in the foreign press, they were never to print them in their own papers. The meeting had its effect. The journalists went away believing that the 'Alpine Redoubt' really existed.

A month later, after the counter-offensive in the Ardennes had failed, Goebbels set up a special journalistic unit to produce stories about the mythical Alpine defence system, stories of impregnable positions, underground supply dumps, élite defence troops, factories built into mountain-sides, etc.

The American newspapers soon took up the story again. The now defunct US illustrated magazine *Colliers*, for instance, ran a detailed article in its January issue about a gigantic guerrilla warfare programme being set up by the Nazis near Bad Aussee, which was close to the Fuehrer's home at Berchtesgaden and in the centre of the 'Redoubt'. According to the American writer the cream of both the SS and the Hitler Youth were being trained for post-war partisan operations in the area. When the Nazis lost the war, a new headquarters would be set up in the Alps somewhere above Bad Aussee (possibly even in a neutral country)[1] from where the 'Werewolves'—the journalist

[1] At this time the Swiss General Staff thought the Germans might invade their country in the moment of defeat and use the Swiss defensive system for a long-term final battle.

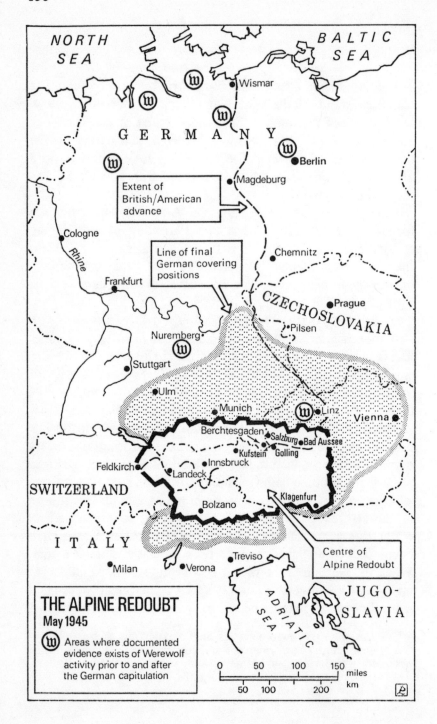

NORTH SEA

BALTIC SEA

•Wismar

G E R M A N Y

•Berlin

•Magdeburg

Extent of
British/American
advance

Cologne

Rhine

•Frankfurt

Line of final
German covering
positions

CZECHOSLOVAKIA

•Prague

•Chemnitz

•Pilsen

Nuremberg•

•Stuttgart

•Ulm

•Munich

•Linz

Vienna

Berchtesgaden•

•Salzburg

•Bad Aussee

•Kufstein

•Golling

Feldkirch•

•Innsbruck

•Landeck

SWITZERLAND

•Bolzano

•Klagenfurt

Centre of
Alpine Redoubt

I T A L Y

•Milan

•Verona

•Treviso

A D R I A T I C   S E A

JUGO-
SLAVIA

THE ALPINE REDOUBT
May 1945

Areas where documented
evidence exists of Werewolf
activity prior to and after
the German capitulation

0   50   100   150 miles

50   100   200 km

already knew the name—under the command of Ernst Kaltenbrunner, head of the German SS Security Police would launch
raids on the Allied occupation forces. Other newspapers followed suit and Allied intelligence started to interest itself in
the 'Alpine Redoubt', although already in the previous September the American OSS[1] unit in Zurich, under the command of
Allen Dulles, had predicted that the Nazis would make a last-
ditch stand in the Bavaria–Austria area.

While press comment in America grew in volume, supported
by such reliable newspapermen and authorities as Drew
Pearson and Victor Schiff who were now maintaining that
'Hitler's henchmen in the east of Switzerland are expected to
make a final stand',[2] both SHAEF Intelligence, under the
British General, Kenneth Strong, and 12th Army Intelligence,
under Brigadier General Sibert, set about investigating the new
threat.

Although General Strong knew that his colleagues in Montgomery's 21st Army Group Intelligence discounted the idea of
an Alpine Redoubt and a period of protracted guerrilla warfare,
he took the threat seriously in the SHAEF Intelligence Summary of 11 March. Discussing the 'National Redoubt', as the
Summary called it, the SHAEF intelligence men maintained that
'accumulated ground information and a limited amount of
photographic evidence now make it possible to give a rather
more definite estimate of the progress of plans for the "last-
ditch stand" of the Nazi Party . . . The main trend of German
defence policy does seem directed primarily to the safeguarding
of the Alpine Zone . . . Air cover shows at least twenty sites
of recent underground activity (as well as numerous natural
caves) mainly in the regions of Feldkirch, Kufstein, Berchtesgaden and Golling, where ground sources have reported
underground accommodation for stores and personnel. The

[1] Office of Strategic Services, forerunner of the CIA.
[2] Schiff's article was based on a German radio broadcast—probably by
Dr Paul Schmidt—which forecast that millions of Germans would wage
guerrilla warfare and kill ten Allied soldiers for every German who died.

existence of several reported underground factories has also been confirmed. In addition, several new barracks and hutted camps have been seen on air photographs, particularly around Innsbruck, Landeck and the Berghof.[1] It thus appears that ground reports of extensive preparations for the accommodation of the German Maquis-to-be are not unfounded.'

Twelve days later General Bradley's 12th Army Group HQ in Belgium issued its reading of the situation, entitled *Reorientation of Strategy*, based on Sibert's researches among German POWs. In his appendix to the report, Bradley maintained that it was now known that there would be guerrilla warfare conducted by the Germans in the Alps under the leadership of the Werewolves and directed from Berchtesgaden.

He pointed out further that the German defensive tactics had changed. The Germans were giving first priority to the use of obstacles in the course of their fighting withdrawal before the advancing Americans, followed by 'concealment, cover, communications, and finally, fields of fire'.

Four days later General Patch's Seventh Army further to the south of Bradley also published its findings on the Redoubt. This report went beyond both the SHAEF and 12th Army Group's interpretation and though it claimed to be based on fairly reliable sources, the Seventh's appraisal continued the wildest rumours. According to the Seventh Army's intelligence men, Himmler had ordered provisions for 100,000 men, and the Alpine fortress was to be defended by eighty crack units. Trains had been reported pouring into the area, carrying new types of cannon. Workshops were being built which were capable of manufacturing a complete Messerschmitt. When everything was ready, some 200,000 veteran SS troops would withdraw into the area and together with the Werewolves—'who were thoroughly imbued with the Nazi spirit'—fight to the last man.

In the great map room near the Supreme Commander's office in Rheims an intelligence chart bearing the legend 'Reported National Redoubt' began to fill up with red marks.

[1] Hitler's mountain-top home at Berchtesgaden.

The map, which detailed some twenty thousand square miles of territory in Bavaria and Austria together with a small part of Northern Italy, was soon covered with a rash of notations, each bearing a military symbol indicating an enemy installation. Food, ammunition, petrol dumps, barracks, bunkers, underground factories and troop silos, zigzagging lines of fortifications and guerrilla concentration points—each fresh day brought new identifications, all of them completely unconfirmed!

Yet both General Eisenhower and his Intelligence Chief, General Strong, felt they had to take them seriously. As Strong commented, speaking to General Bedell Smith, 'The redoubt may not be there, but we have to take steps to prevent it being there.'

Bedell Smith agreed. There was, in his opinion, 'every reason to believe that the Nazis intend to make their last stand among the crags.'

In fact, the British General, who had been military attaché in Berlin before the war and knew the German military hierarchy, was more cautious. He did not swallow all of the Seventh Army Report, yet he could not discount it either. In February one of the American intelligence sections had captured a German document stating that the Werewolves must recruit 'men of outstanding ability, experience and courage . . . for its leaders,' and the capture of a Werewolves headquarters in Southern Germany convinced him that if the Allies did not advance soon, then the Germans would be in a position to set up 'a widespread network of Resistance posts which might well . . . interfere with our operations.'

All week Eisenhower wrestled with the problem. The last water barrier defending the remaining German territory was being crossed. The question was now, in which direction should his armies advance? On to Berlin, or southwards towards the Alpine Redoubt?

But Eisenhower's headache was not only occasioned by the problem of enemy resistance. There were also human problems involving his own top generals, namely General Bradley,

Commander of the 12th Army Group and General Montgomery, his British equivalent for the 21st Army Group. The
feud between these two generals was long-standing; its origins
can probably be traced back to the early days of the campaign
in Brittany. However, the real trouble had started when in
December, 1944, at the height of the Ardennes crisis, Eisenhower had handed over command of Bradley's 1st Army to the
British soldier. Thus, during the Battle of the Bulge, an almost
exclusively American battle, a British general commanded
more US troops—the 1st and 9th US Armies—than the American ground commander, General Bradley.

If that were not enough of a blow to Bradley's ego, Montgomery reopened the wound by his controversial press conference of 7 January, 1945, in which he summed up the 'lessons'
of the battle. In that completely self-assured, almost unthinking
manner of his which so angered American officers (one officer
described his take-over of the 1st US Army like 'Christ come to
cleanse the temple'), Montgomery told reporters that 'As soon
as I saw what was happening I took certain steps myself to
ensure that *if* the Germans got to the Meuse they would
certainly not get over that river. And I carried out certain
movements so as to provide balanced dispositions to meet the
threatened danger; these were, at the time, merely precautions,
i.e. I was thinking ahead.'

And thus the interview had gone on with the repeated empha-
sis on 'I' and *not one reference* to Bradley, whose troops he
was using.

The details of the interview, received in a doctored German
version over what his staff supposed was the BBC but which in
actual fact was a German station, had enraged the usually
even-tempered Omar Bradley. After issuing his own unauthorized statement in which he categorically stated that
Montgomery's command of American troops was only tem-
porary, he had demanded an interview with the Supreme
Commander.

Raising the question of the apparent blow to his prestige

that the transfer of command had made, he had told General Eisenhower 'you must know after what has happened I cannot serve under Montgomery. If he is to be put in command of all ground forces, you must send me home, for if Montgomery goes in over me, I will have lost the confidence of my command.'

In addition, Eisenhower knew that Bradley's most famous Army commander, the hot-tempered Patton of the Third Army, would probably follow suit if Montgomery were given the plum job of overall Allied ground commander.[1]

Eisenhower knew that if he continued his advance all the way to Berlin, the British general would have the kudos of the final victory and the prize of Berlin to boot. That would be something which Bradley would not tolerate; and there was always public opinion to be considered back home. If, however, he stopped Montgomery's drive in the North, giving him the River Elbe as his stop-line, then he would have the resources to let General Bradley carry out the final great campaign in the South.

In 12th Army Group's Reorientation of Strategy of 25 March, Bradley had written that Allied objectives had changed, rendering 'obsolete the plans we brought with us over the beaches'. The significance of Berlin, according to Bradley, was very much diminished. In fact, 'the metropolitan area can no longer occupy a position of importance . . . all indications suggest that the enemy's political and military directorate is already in the process of displacing to the "Redoubt" in lower Bavaria.'

Now Bradley suggested that instead of making a thrust to the north, his army group should split Germany in two by driving through the centre. This would 'prevent German forces from withdrawing' towards the south and 'into the Redoubt'. Moreover, once this move had been successfully executed, the Twelfth Army Group would swing south to reduce any remaining resistance in the Alpine Redoubt.

[1] When Bradley told Patton of his threat to resign, the latter had put his arm round his boss's shoulder and said, 'If you quit, Brad, then I'll be quitting with you'.

We know that General Eisenhower took the Werewolves and the Alpine Redoubt seriously enough that spring. In his memoirs he writes, 'If the German was permitted to establish the Redoubt he might possibly force us to engage in a long-drawn-out guerrilla type of warfare, or a costly siege. Thus he could keep alive his desperate hope that through disagreement among the Allies he might yet be able to secure terms more favourable than those of unconditional surrender. The evidence was clear that the Nazi intended to make the attempt . . .

'Another Nazi purpose, somewhat akin to that of establishing a mountain fortress, was the organization of an underground army, to which he gave the significant name of "Werewolves". The purpose of the Werewolf organization, which was to be composed only of loyal followers of Hitler, was murder and terrorism. Boys and girls as well as adults were to be absorbed into the secret organization with the hope of so terrifying the countryside and making so difficult the problem of occupation that the conquering forces would presumably be glad to get out.

'The way to stop this project—and such a development was always a possibility because of the passionate devotion to their Fuehrer of so many young Germans—was to overrun the entire national territory before its organization could be effected.'

But all the same the personality problem and its effect on American public opinion also weighed heavily on his mind. There are some unkind critics of the Supreme Commander (especially in the American camp) who maintain that Eisenhower was already considering a political career in those weeks of the war, and that he was only too concerned that his 'press' back home was good.[1]

[1] General Patton, with surprising foresight, had predicted in March, 1945, that Eisenhower would be President one day, stating cynically that the only reason that Ike had come to visit him and his army was because his men represented 'a lot of votes'. R. Ingersoll, former newspaper editor and Bradley's aide, makes the same point, remarking about Eisenhower's concern with publicity at that time, 'The big parades in New York and Washington were closer than they had been six months before.'

Though perhaps this is going too far, it certainly was true that Eisenhower was intensely concerned about the kind of publicity he received in the United States. And in the end his concern with publicity won the day. In the final days of March, 1945, the 4,000 to 5,000 enthusiastic, fanatical young men and women still training in their secret Werewolf schools and the undefended, unarmed Alpine Fortress became the two most decisive factors in the determination of future Allied strategy in Germany, and as a result, helped to change the whole face of Europe.

III

Half an hour before midnight, Ilse Hirsch shook Heidorn out of a fevered sleep. The guide started anxiously and his hand reached automatically for his pistol. But it was gone.

'What—My pistol, it's not there,' he stuttered, staring up at the woman's pale face.

Ilse ignored his unspoken question. Later he guessed the others had taken the weapon with them. 'They've still not come back,' she whispered, 'And I don't think they're coming back.'

Heidorn suddenly was wide awake. 'What shall we do?' he breathed. Ilse's brow creased in a worried frown. 'I don't like to leave them. It's not comradely,[1] but I don't think we can wait any longer.'

'You're right, Ilse.'

'Do you think you can guide us to the Rhine?'

'Of course,' Heidorn answered. It was what he had been longing for ever since they had jumped from the aeroplane. 'Come on, let's get started.'

Ilse shook the boy awake. 'We're getting out of here—*now*!' He sprang to his feet and joined them in the nervous packing

---

[1] 'Comradely' was a favourite word of hers and long after the war she had used it to describe her relationship with her fellow Werewolves and her whole attitude to the Nazi movement.

158

of their bundles. They scattered the bits and pieces of the equipment which they could not take with them around their camp. (These were found afterwards by American patrols.) They were just about to disappear into the trees when they heard the sound of someone or something blundering through the undergrowth near by.

Heidorn and Ilse stared at each other in shock. Heidorn for a moment hoped it might be a deer. (Since the start of the war, with no hunting allowed, the deer had multiplied rapidly in the forests of the border area.) But no deer made that much noise. The boy drew his pistol.

Then they heard a voice they recognized immediately. 'It's me,' the thick Austrian accent was unmistakable—it was Sepp. He had burst through the trees, his pistol in one hand and what looked like a piece of cloth in the other. His chest was heaving with the effort of running and he was sweating profusely.

'Where are the others?' Ilse demanded.

Sepp shook his head, still trying to catch his breath. 'Killed— captured . . . bumped into *Ami* patrol . . . fired on us . . . I . . . I . . . got separated from them . . . They're behind me.'

His words confirmed their fears. Hardly giving Leitgeb time to seize his own bundle, they had fled into the surrounding trees, heading for the thick forests of the Eifel, away from the city and the enemy soldiers now searching for them.

They broke camp on Sunday the 25th and marched through the Eifel forest all night. As they marched, Sepp regained his composure, and he told them that Wenzel had turned out to be a cowardly pig and had been too scared to kill the traitor; in the end he had been forced to seize the pistol from him and do the job himself. As proof he showed them a pair of grey cloth gloves he had taken off the dead man and an armband with two words written on it in English.[1] He explained that the chief burgomaster had been wearing the band on his arm as an

---

[1] 'Town Mayor'.

indication that he had official permission to be on the streets after curfew time. With a laugh, he put it on and commented, 'If we bump into an *Ami* patrol, I'll tell them that I'm the burgomaster of the nearest village and they'll let us go on.'

On the 26th they spent the afternoon resting in a typical Eifel shooting blind, a tower-like construction set on spindly legs at the edge of a wood so that the hunter could watch the game unobserved. The rickety board-and-wattle construction was cold and draughty and it was so cramped that they could not stretch out to rest, but it was an ideal hiding place, giving them a good view of all possible ways of approach. Towards evening Heidorn clambered stiffly down the broken wooden ladder and went into the forest to check their position. When he returned some minutes later he shook his head at their inquiring looks. 'No, I give up.'

The others looked at him dumbly. He meant that he couldn't find the way to the hunting lodge near the border where he had arranged to meet Hennemann if the group broke up.

'What now?' Morgenschweiss asked. The guide shrugged. 'We'll go on alone to the Rhine as planned. I know a place where we can hide for a few days and then when we're rested, we'll cross the Rhine.'

'How far is it?' Sepp asked.

Again Heidorn shrugged. 'I'd guess perhaps one or two nights march from here. It depends on how much ground we can cover in one night.' Sepp nodded slowly as he absorbed the news. Then he flexed his big shoulders. 'All right then, we'd better get going.'

They marched on all night, hardly giving themselves a break, with Heidorn in the lead and Morgenschweiss bringing up the rear. Towards morning as the first light of the new day began to tinge the horizon, Heidorn stopped them.

For a moment, he scanned the bare fields ahead of them. Barely visible to the south, they could make out a small village, with the thick double-onion of a Baroque church tower sticking bleakly into the sky. 'I think, I know where we are,' Heidorn said slowly. 'Near Simonskall. You see that stream down there—it's the Kall.'

Leitgeb rubbed his eyes. 'Well, come on, let's get going. We can do a bit more before the locals get up. Let's skirt that village and then find a place to hide up for the day.'

Slowly they set off again. The days of hiding and marching without proper food were beginning to take their toll. Ilse felt she would give anything for a soft clean bed in which she could collapse and sleep and sleep for ever.

They worked their way carefully round the village and no one spotted them. Apart from the occasional dog barking and the sound of cows lowing in their barns, the village might well have been completely deserted. And, indeed, many of the pathetically poor Eifel villages were depopulated or inhabited only by old people who had not gone off to the war.

They had just left the village behind and spotted the dull white wall of the dam which Heidorn identified as the *Dreilagerbachtalssperre* when it happened. Leitgeb had strayed out some fifty metres to their left, picking his way through the damp grass. Suddenly there was a huge explosion. The field heaved and an enormous fresh brown lump of earth was thrown into the air, as if some gigantic mole were at work beneath it. There was a flash of red and yellow and a fraction of a second later the hot wave of the explosion struck them, sending them reeling back. Someone screamed. The scream ended in a gurgle of pain. Overhead a panic-stricken flight of black crows rose into the sky from the nearby trees squawking in protest at the sudden disturbance. Then silence.

'*Ach Du. Mein Gott*!' cried Heidorn. His face was deathly pale, staring rigidly to the spot where Leitgeb had been standing a moment before. But now the Austrian was no longer standing. Instead he lay slumped awkwardly in a pile of fresh brown earth which was still smoking.

'A mine—we're in a minefield!' Morgenschweiss cried.

Ilse felt a cold wave of shock—a minefield!

Heidorn took charge. He had been in minefields before.

Not moving a foot, he swung round to Morgenschweiss. 'Don't get scared,' he called. 'No need to be afraid. They're way down below the surface. It was his weight that did it.'

'Is he dead?' Ilse asked.

'I don't know, but we've got to get his papers off him. If they've got the others and then find him we're for it. They'll know we're still alive.'

'Shall I go and see?' Morgenschweiss broke the silence which followed the guide's words.

Ilse was amazed at the boy's courage.

'All right,' Heidorn said, grateful that the youngster had volunteered for a task he would otherwise have had to undertake himself. 'Just walk lightly towards him. Keep your eyes on the grass. If you see anything sticking up, stop and I'll tell you what to do.'

Morgenschweiss bit his bottom lip like a small boy does in moments of hesitation, but he said nothing. Instead he began to move forward slowly to where Leitgeb's body lay.

Tensely Ilse watched him inch his way forward. In spite of the coldness of the morning, she could feel the warmth of the perspiration on her forehead; but she dared not even move her hand to wipe it way. It was like being at the circus watching the climax of a highwire act. One unnecessary move, a sudden cough, a nervous laugh from the tense audience and the artiste might come hurtling down to his death.

But Morgenschweiss made it. Carefully the boy knelt down next to Leitgeb with his back towards them. He seemed to remain in this attitude of prayer for a long time, then carefully he began to break off branches from a nearby bush, kneeling all the time, and placing them over the body. Leitgeb was dead.

Moments later he was with them again, wiping his hands free of the sticky resin. 'The whole side of his face is gone. He's dead all right, poor Sepp.'

Heidorn did not reply. He did not even look at the body while Morgenschweiss spoke. His eyes were searching the fields, from which the damp now began to rise as the rays of the sun grew warmer. He was praying that no one had heard the noise of the explosion. If they had, it would not be the civilians who would come to look. It would be the *Amis*.

'Come on,' he said urgently, 'we'd better get out of here quick!'

Swiftly they turned and, following in Heidorn's footsteps, went back the way they had come. While the body of the man who had killed the Chief Burgomaster began to stiffen beneath its hiding place of twigs and leaves, Aachen prepared to bury Franz Oppenhoff.

IV

On 27 March, General Eisenhower received a message from his 'boss' in Washington, General George Marshall. The message read, 'From the current operations report, it looks like the German defence system in the west may break up. This would permit you to move a considerable number of divisions rapidly eastwards on a broad front. What are your views on pushing US forces rapidly forward on, say, the Nuremberg-Linz or Karlsruhe-Munich axes? The idea behind this is that . . . rapid action might prevent the formation of organized resistance areas. The mountainous country in the south is considered a possibility for one of these.'

It was this cable that finally determined Eisenhower's plan for the further conduct of the war in Central Europe. The next day his proposals were sent to Mr Churchill in London, to General Marshall, the US Chief of Staff in Washington and to Generalissimo Joseph Stalin in Moscow.

In his cable to Stalin, Eisenhower pointed out that 'My immediate operations are designed to encircle and destroy the enemy defending the Ruhr. I estimate that this phase will end late in April or even earlier, and my task will be to divide the remaining forces by joining with your forces. The best axis on which to effect this junction would be Erfurt-Leipzig-Dresden. This is the area to which main German Government departments are being moved. It is along this axis that I propose to make my main effort. In addition, as soon as possible, a secondary advance will be made to effect junction with your forces in the area Regensburg-Linz, thereby preventing the consolidation of German resistance in the Redoubt in southern Germany.'

It was a point that he reiterated to Marshall in another cable which he dispatched on the evening of the 28th. Mentioning the latter's fears of a 'National Redoubt', he commented that he too was aware of the 'importance of forestalling the possibilities of the enemy forming organized resistance areas' and would 'make a drive towards Linz and Munich as soon as circumstances allowed'.

Although he was still worried by the Alpine Redoubt, or 'Mountain Citadel' as he called it, Eisenhower now felt he had finally got things under control again. By way of an afterthought he pencilled on the draft of a cable to Montgomery his last official act of that fateful day, 'As you say, the situation looks good.' He little realized how bad the situation really was.

The situation of the fugitive killers was not much better. Late on that afternoon of 28 March, Heidorn guided them round the little town of Schleiden, led them through the woods towards the tiny hamlet of Olef and into further trouble.

Ilse Hirsch was patiently plodding her way through the thick undergrowth just to Heidorn's right when she stumbled. There was a sudden sheet of flame, followed by a thick crump and he felt a heavy blow on the arm. As he fell, gasping with pain, he realized that Ilse had blundered against a trip wire attached to a mine. No one could have laid a regular minefield in the thick undergrowth.

They had all been hit. Morgenschweiss in the back and hand, Ilse in the right knee.

Morgenschweiss, as usual, was the first to react. The boy struggled to his feet, his black jacket staining rapidly with blood. 'I've been hit! They've got me in the back.'

'Shut up,' Heidorn said. 'You're not the only one.' He staggered over to where Ilse Hirsch lay on the heap of fresh earth thrown up by the mine.

Her face was paler than ever and she was bleeding profusely. 'Can you get up?' he asked. Ilse held a hand pressed tightly around her knee and peered at the thick black blood welling from beneath the torn trouser-leg. Numbly she shook her head.

'Come on,' he said, 'take my hand and try it.'

He stretched out his hand and helped her to her feet. The strain made the sweat stand out in tiny pearls along her hairline. She shook her head. 'I can't do it.'

Slowly Heidorn let her down again. For what seemed a long time Morgenschweiss and Heidorn looked down at her on the ground, her hands clasped round her knee, trying to stop the blood. But it wouldn't stop.

Morgenschweiss looked at Heidorn. 'What are we going to do with her?' Heidorn did not answer.

Ilse stared with horrified fascination at her leg as if she could not believe that this terrible thing had happened to her.

She formed her words carefully, rounding her mouth in the way that children do when they are learning to speak. 'You'd better go . . . You can leave me here . . . When you're well away . . . I'll call out . . . Perhaps someone will come out and find me.'

Heidorn knew that there was no hope of anyone finding her until daybreak. It was already getting dark and soon it would be curfew. The farmers would already be back in their villages, locking up their barns and stables for the night. She would have to spend at least twelve hours in the open before anyone found her—and even in daylight there would not be too many farmers who would wander off the beaten track to where she lay; they too knew about the danger of the mines.

Heidorn looked across at Morgenschweiss. But the youth, his hand clasped to his injured back, dropped his eyes. He did not want to have to help decide what they should do next.

Ilse moved herself slowly until her back was propped against a tree. 'You'd better go,' she said again. 'Go now.' She waved a blood-stained hand at the two men.

'All right, Ilse,' Heidorn said, bending down and touching her hand. 'We'll be getting along.'

'*Alles gute*,'[1] Morgenschweiss said, idiotically, unable to find words to convey the finality of that moment.

Slowly they turned and began to make their way carefully through the darkening wood, their eyes fixed firmly and anxiously on the ground searching for mines.

For Ilse it was all over. Her 'comrades' had left her. With a feeling akin to despair she watched them get further and further away. If they would only look back, she told herself. But they didn't. They disappeared out of sight and she was alone.

The next day she was found. A farmer heard weak cries coming from the forest in the early hours of the morning. He stopped his wagon and, tying up his old nag, went to investigate. There he came upon the exhausted Ilse, propped up against a tree in a pool of blood. For her it was the end of the mission, but there was no let up as yet for the other two Were-wolves.

Hour after hour they marched across the rugged Eifel country-side, anxiously skirting each sad little village they came to, hurrying on with relief once they were safely on the other side. But their pace was beginning to lag. Morgenschweiss started to drop further and further behind and though Heidorn waited for him to catch up, he could see that the boy was about finished. His face had become deathly white—like those of the men whom Heidorn had seen dying in the Ardennes. He realized Morgenschweiss could not go on much further.

They had just worked their way round the little village of Kall when they first became aware of the noise of fast-flowing water.

'What's that?' Morgenschweiss said, stumbling on behind Heidorn.

'It's the River Erft,' Heidorn said.

[1] 'All the best.'

The boy wiped the sweat from his face. 'Do we have to cross it?'

Heidorn nodded.

A few minutes later they were on the bank of the river. Heidorn knew that for most of the year the river could be crossed very easily. But now with the long hard winter, the worst in Europe for thirty years, it had become an angry, raging torrent.

While Morgenschweiss sank wearily to the ground, Heidorn scrambled down the bank, cupped his hand and took a drink of the ice-cold water. He crouched down and surveyed the stretch of rushing water for a good spot to cross. Then he turned to look at the boy who lay on the wet grass, his eyes closed, one arm thrown over his face, as if he wanted to blot out the whole world and its problems.

Heidorn got to his feet and climbed back up to where Morgenschweiss was lying. 'Come on,' he said sharply.

Shakily, Morgenschweiss got to his feet and with Heidorn holding onto his arm went down to the water. With Heidorn's aid he successfully negotiated the slippery boulders at the edge of the water, but as soon as he felt the strong tug of the current around his legs, he panicked. 'I can't do it,' he cried 'I can't swim that! I'll drown!'

Violently he pulled himself free and struggled back to the shore, the water dripping from his legs. A moment later he had fallen to the ground again. '*Ich bin fertig*', he moaned '*Ich kann nicht mehr*.'[1]

Momentarily oblivious of the water tearing at his legs, the guide stood there in the river staring at the beaten youth. He knew that Morgenschweiss was telling the truth. He was finished. 'All right, Erich, I'll leave you here. When I've got away you can call for help. Somebody should come along soon.'

Morgenschweiss did not even answer. Heidorn took one last look at the boy then he turned and plunged into the water, getting deeper and deeper until he was swimming, fighting for

[1] I'm finished. I can't go on.

his life, all thoughts of Erich Morgenschweiss gone from his mind. There was only one of them left now.[1]

In the early hours of the morning of Sunday, 1 April, Easter Sunday, Heidorn struggled up the long steep entrance to the lonely *Gut Hombusch* landhouse which had been the headquarters of his old unit in the winter of 1944.

Gut Hombusch was situated a couple of miles from the village of Mechernich, on the top of a steep, well-wooded hill, completely hidden from the road and, indeed, from all sides. It was a perfect hideout and the exhausted guide intended to rest there until he was fit enough to carry on to the Rhine.[2]

Cautiously Heidorn approached the house, which although it was built in the early twentieth century looked, with its steep slate turrets and immensely thick walls, as if it dated back to the times of the medieval robber barons. As he staggered up the entrance road, he saw that the slit trenches dug into the verges had been hastily abandoned. He guessed, therefore, that there were no German troops left in the house. But if there were any *Amis* about he would have seen their transport; he knew the *Amis* always drove everywhere. Yet there were no jeeps or trucks about, nor were there even tracks in the deep mud on the road leading up to the building.

Nevertheless the house was inhabited by someone. He could tell that by the smoke which curled up from the tall chimney. Perhaps Baron Solemacher, the bailiff, whom he remembered

---

[1] Erich Morgenschweiss was found soon afterwards by a Frau Sülz, who threw away his pistol and had him carried into the catholic hospital in the nearby village of Vussem, to which Ilse Hirsch had also been taken. But Ilse soon developed pneumonia due to exposure and was moved to another hospital before Morgenschweiss became aware that she was in the same place.

[2] Because of the natural reticence of all those connected with the Werewolf organization, I have not been able to establish whether Heidorn knew at that time that less than two hundred yards from the entrance to the landhouse there was a secret Werewolf munitions dump, filled with mines, explosives, etc., which when it was destroyed after the war left a crater covering a quarter of an acre.

from the days when he had been stationed there, had remained to protect his precious paintings and antique furniture.

Summoning up the last of his strength, he entered the yard. Cautiously remaining close to the walls, he crept from window to window in the inner courtyard, listening intently for any sound. But the house seemed dead and abandoned. Everywhere there were signs of a hurried flight by the German troops who had last occupied the place. Bits and pieces of equipment were scattered all around and through the open door of one of the sheds he saw abandoned greatcoats and gasmasks which he recognized as having once belonged to his former unit. Then, suddenly, he heard a voice. It seemed to be coming from the direction of the kitchen. Heidorn hurried towards the sound. Crouching under the kitchen window, he twisted his head to one side so that he could hear better.

There was someone in there! And whoever it was was speaking German!

A wave of relief surged through him as he recognized the speaker. There was no mistaking that accent with its trace of a lisp. The speaker was *SS Untersturmbannführer* Herbert Wenzel. He was talking to Hennemann.

V

Eisenhower's cable to Winston Churchill, informing the Prime Minister that he had decided to halt at the Elbe and not take Berlin, in order to concentrate on reducing the 'Alpine Redoubt' because of the danger it presented as a stronghold for the Werewolf movement, exploded like a bombshell in London. Churchill and his advisers did not believe either in the Redoubt or in the German intention to fight a protracted guerrilla war after their defeat in battle. For the British Prime Minister, the capture of Berlin was the primary strategic objective of the rest of the war in Europe. As he wrote to Eisenhower on

2 April, 'I deem it highly important that we should shake hands with the Russians as far to the east as possible.'

But Eisenhower did not share Churchill's suspicion of the Russians. As Churchill was later to write in his memoirs, 'In his generous instincts, in his love of laughter, in his devotion to a comrade and in his healthy, direct outlook on the affairs of workaday life, "the Russian" seemed to bear a marked similarity to . . . the average American.' He was totally unconcerned, as a result, with the political impact of his decision. Berlin was not worth the cost of 100,000 American lives, which Bradley, only too eager to ensure that his own operations southwards would be approved, assured him it would need to take the German capital.

Throughout the Easter weekend, angry cables flew back and forth across the Atlantic, attacking and defending the controversial Eisenhower decision. The British Chiefs-of-Staff sent a harsh message to their American counterparts complaining about the Eisenhower decision. As Sir Alan Brooke noted in his diary for 29 March, 'To start with, he (Eisenhower) has no business to address Stalin direct, his communications should be through the Combined Chiefs of Staff; secondly, he produced a telegram which was unintelligible; and finally, what was implied in it appeared to be entirely adrift and a change from all that had been previously agreed upon.' In their message to General Marshal, the British Chiefs pointed out that their Intelligence did not believe the rumours about the Alpine Redoubt, and should not be considered as a factor on which to base future strategy.

Marshall's reaction was to send a wire to Eisenhower asking for further details of his plan and to General Deane, American military representative in Moscow, telling him to stop delivery of the Eisenhower cable to Stalin.

While this was going on, Churchill himself got on the scrambler phone to Eisenhower just before midnight on 29 March and, carefully avoiding any mention of the cable to Stalin, asked Eisenhower to consider the strategic importance of Berlin in his future decisions. Eisenhower said he would think about it.

The next day Eisenhower replied by cable, and again to Churchill it seemed that Eisenhower's thinking revealed a complete lack of understanding of the potential post-war menace presented by Soviet Russia. Churchill still stuck to his idea of driving eastwards to 'join hands with the Russians or to attain the general line of the Elbe'.

On that same day the British Chiefs-of-Staff received an answer to their wire to Marshall. It stated flatly that Eisenhower was 'the best judge of the measures which offer the earliest prospect of destroying the German Armies of their power to resist,' and that his strategic concept was 'sound from the overall viewpoint of crushing Germany as expeditiously as possible and should receive full support'. In London, an irate Churchill, angry both at his own Chiefs-of-Staff because of their unauthorized cable to Marshall and at Eisenhower because of his equally unauthorized communication to Stalin, realized that the Americans were solidly, even aggressively, behind the European Supreme Commander.

Eisenhower, meanwhile, grew steadily angrier at the trans-Atlantic interchange of messages about his decision. He had expected some angry reaction from London because he had cut Montgomery's role in future operations, but he had not bargained with the British attitude to his cable to Stalin. He believed his action had been correct and militarily essential.

The world knew Eisenhower only from the newsreel photographs. The man in the street thought of him as the 'general with the smile', and 'good old Ike'. But 'good old Ike' had a hair-trigger temper, as many of his intimate associates knew to their cost. Now he lost it completely. In a detailed cable he sent to Marshall on the morning of 30 March, he stated, 'Merely following the principle that Field-Marshal Brooke has always shouted to me, I am determined to concentrate on one major thrust . . . Afterwards we can launch a movement to the south—eastward to prevent Nazi occupation of the mountain citadel.'

For him the 'mountain citadel' had become more important than Berlin, whatever Churchill said to the contrary.

'May I point out,' he wrote, 'that Berlin itself is no longer a particularly important objective. Its usefulness to the Germans has been largely destroyed and even his government is preparing to move to another area' (i.e. the Alpine Redoubt).

By the time Ike reached his final paragraph his anger at the British reaction to his plan was clearly visible. 'The Prime Minister and his Chiefs-of-Staff opposed "Anvil"[1]; they opposed my idea that the Germans should be destroyed west of the Rhine before we made our great effort across the river; and they insisted that the route leading northeastwards from Frankfurt would involve us merely in slow, rough-country fighting. Now they apparently want me to turn aside on operations in which would be involved many thousands of troops before the German forces are fully defeated. I submit that these things are studied daily and hourly by me and my advisers and that we are animated by one single thought which is the early winning of this war.'[2]

His cable had the desired effect. On Sunday, 1 April, Eisenhower received a cable from the American Chiefs-of-Staff which made their position quite clear. It read, 'The battle of Germany is now at the point where the Commander in the Field is the best judge of the measures which offer the earliest prospect of destroying the German armies or their power to resist . . . General Eisenhower should continue to be free to communicate with the Commander-in-Chief of the Soviet Army.'

Ike had won. He had received the unqualified support of his military superiors back in Washington and he was free to go ahead with his plan. The big question now was—How big a threat were the Werewolves? Would they now start retreating

---

[1] The Invasion of southern France in the autumn of 1944.

[2] It is interesting to note that the 1,000-word cable to Marshall does not appear in General Eisenhower's own *Crusade in Europe* as above. It has been cut and edited, with the phrase 'always shouted to me' changed to 'always emphasized' and the last paragraph dropped altogether.

to the Alpine Redoubt to start a last-ditch defence of the mountainous area?

VI

On 20 April, 1945, General Patton set off in his unarmed Piper Cub to fly to the headquarters of his III Corps which was spear-heading his Army's drive toward the Alpine Redoubt. The general did not believe either in the Alpine Redoubt or in the reported German resistance movement which was supposed to be using it as a base. 'It's a lot of baloney, like the cries of Werewolf', he snorted when his Intelligence officers mentioned the subject.

But if Patton did not take the Werewolves seriously, his staff officers did. At his headquarters the rumour was going round since the assassination of Oppenhoff that the German resistance organization intended to launch glider raids on the Third Army with the intention of murdering high-ranking officers, beginning with the Army Commander himself. They insisted that whenever Patton ventured out to inspect his men in the field he should be accompanied by a heavily armoured car, and his principal aide, Colonel Codman, had been warned to keep a guard on his boss during daylight hours. Patton laughed at his staff officers' fears but in the end he, too, became convinced of the danger and began sleeping with a loaded carbine close at hand.

But on that fine spring afternoon as the General's Piper Cub began to lose height for its approach to Reidfeld Field no one suspected trouble from the Werewolf or any other quarter. Flying behind his boss's plane in a second Cub Colonel Charles Codman yawned lazily. It had been a long busy day so far, but everything was going smoothly. The General was in a good mood, the war was going well and he was satisfied with his commanders. While the planes had been warming up for their last hop of the day, he had told Codman in one of his rare expansive moods, 'I have certainly been lucky in having such corps commanders. Eddy, Walker, Middleton, Van Fleet— all great soldiers.'

Then suddenly it happened. The General's Cub was about two miles from Reidfeld Field, when a fighter plane dived out of the sun. As it flashed by Patton's Cub, there was a chatter of machine guns. Five hundred yards away in the second Cub Codman could see the violet crackle of light along the fighter plane's wings. The fighter was a Spitfire. He was sure of that. He could recognize the typical broad wing. And there were the horizontal white stripes on its fuselage which identified it as an Allied plane. Somehow the Germans had captured it and were using it for their murder mission.

Now the fighter zoomed up and into the sun. For a moment it disappeared. Then it came roaring down again. Patton's pilot tried to lose height and lure the Spitfire close to the ground where it might crash. Again as the fighter dived past the Cub, its machine guns opened up. But the fighter pilot missed his mark once more.

Meanwhile, Patton, clearly outlined in the perspex glass dome of the unarmed spotter plane, was struggling to free his camera and aim it at the fighter.[1] 'What a man!' thought Codman and then swallowed his admiration. The Spitfire was coming in once again.

By now both Cubs were very low, skipping over wooden fences, dipping into hollows and skirting tree tops. With a terrific whining scream, the fighter came roaring at them, its guns chattering. Codman could distinctly see the heat haze ripple along the wing and the dark helmeted outline of the pilot, as the Spitfire rushed by them less than fifty yards away. Again he missed. But this time he had come too low. In his eagerness he had followed the leading Cub down to an altitude from which there was no recovery. At nearly five hundred

[1] Patton lost his traditional cool-headed bravery in this particular instance. Keen as he was to photograph the 'murder plane,' in his nervousness he forgot to take off the camera-cover.

miles an hour, the Spitfire hit the knoll of a hill. Like a flat stone skidding across the surface of a still pond the 'murder plane' flew across the grass a few feet above the ground. Then it slewed round and exploded with a great roar. A grey-white cloud of smoke shot upwards and the Spitfire disintegrated. A few moments later both Cubs landed safely. It was Patton's closest call of the war.

When Colonel Codman had checked that Patton was all right, a search party was sent to look for the wreckage of the plane that had attacked them. It was soon confirmed that the plane was a Spitfire complete with British markings. The news was flashed to III Corps Headquarters and for half-an-hour rumours ran riot in the excited HQ.

But within the hour the mystery was cleared up. The Spitfire had been manned by a Polish volunteer with the RAF who had mistakenly flown out of his own sector. Spotting the two Cubs, which presumably he had not recognized, he had attacked them and sacrificed his own life in a tragic mistake.

The initial hysteria caused by the incident confirmed General Patton in his belief that the Werewolves and their Alpine Redoubt were the figments of some nervous staff officer's imagination, either back in Bradley's HQ or at SHAEF. General van Fleet's III Corps was making swift progress through Bavaria and its commander was confident that he would be on the Danube within a matter of days, or even hours. Now the great Third Army, with 600,000 men, was taking fewer than a hundred casualties a day as it drove into the Redoubt and most of these were caused (in the General's opinion) by young soldiers trying to drive jeeps as if they were tanks, and getting themselves killed in the process. As he wrote himself after the war, 'Considering that at this time the Third Army had fourteen divisions in action and an equivalent number of corp and army troops, one gets an idea of how cheap the fighting was.'

But if General Patton whose Army, with that of General Patch (the US Seventh Army), was now finding that the Redoubt did not exist save in the minds of the staff, General Bedell Smith, Eisenhower's Chief-of-Staff was still not convinced that he and his boss had been misled.

The day after Patton's close shave, Bedell Smith called an 'off-the-record' press conference, in which he went over Eisenhower's reasons for not advancing towards Berlin. Then he went on to discuss the Alpine Redoubt. He told the assembled correspondents that Intelligence really knew very little of the last-ditch fortification, but 'we are beginning to think it will be a lot more than we will expect.' Pointing out that the Alpine Redoubt would probably be very heavily fortified, he said that Berlin held no significance any more, 'not anything comparable to that of the so-called national redoubt'.

Asked how Patton and Patch would set about reducing the Nazi fortification, he answered that he didn't think the job would be too hard. Perhaps conventional fighting might last a month, but it would be followed by a prolonged period of guerrilla warfare. There was a 'helluva lot of pressure from Washington' to redeploy troops to the Pacific war so that although Eisenhower might declare a victory in Europe, guerrilla warfare in the remote Alps could go on for weeks— even for months—after the Redoubt itself had collapsed. This 'mass of manpower (i.e. German), ill-trained and ill-assorted as much of it was, held the possibility of prolonged resistance, particularly if it could gain the crags and canyons in the south, the site of the National Redoubt.'

When Correspondent Drew Middleton of the *New York Times* left the conference his previous feeling that the war was all over bar the shouting had vanished. Sitting down at his desk in the press room he began to write his article for his paper. Bearing in mind Bedell Smith's warning that the information was 'off the record', he commenced his daily chore guardedly. But when he was finished it was obvious to the dullest reader that Drew Middleton thought that the reduction of the National Redoubt was Eisenhower's major military problem. It might necessitate a full-scale military campaign carried out not only by the two American Armies, the Third and Seventh, but also by the Russians coming up from Austria.

VII

The very day that Bedell Smith gave his press conference, Hitler's most intelligent and capable Minister, Albert Speer, drove out of besieged Berlin determined to do something about the new resistance movement.

Speer had been shaken out of his hero-worship for the Fuehrer by the latter's 'New Orders'. These instructions which had just been issued by Hitler threatened to reduce Germany to ruins if they were carried out. At first Speer set out to murder Hitler, using poisoned gas, but this plan came to nothing. He subsequently decided systematically to sabotage the 'Nero Orders'. As part of this decision, he realized, he had to put a stop to the Werewolves, for if they started operating in the Allies' rear, there was no knowing what kind of reprisals the Allies might take against the beaten German Nation.

To this end Speer composed what he called a 'rebel's speech!' which urged resistance against the 'Nero Orders'. Soldiers should resist any order to destroy bridges, factories, railways and the like 'with all possible means, if necessary by the use of firearms'. In addition, Speer called upon villagers to surrender their villages without any attempt at defence and not to take part in Werewolf activities. In fact, the Werewolf should be banned immediately.

At the same time, Speer scribbled a hasty note to Dr Richard Fischer, general manager of the Berlin Electricity Works, ordering him to discontinue supplies of power to the German radio station at Königswusterhausen from which Goebbels' fanatical *Radio Werwolf* broadcasts emanated. Once, however, the Russians were within spitting distance of this, Germany's most powerful radio station, he intended to broadcast his 'rebel speech' as *Radio Werwolf's* last official act. By so doing, he hoped that those who were still resisting would believe that they had been *ordered* to stop their guerrilla activities which could only bring disaster for Germany.

A week later Speer hurried to Hamburg to see Gauleiter Kaufmann, who had surrounded himself with well-armed students from the University and had assured Speer, whose opinion of the Werewolves he shared, 'Here you're safe. We can depend on my men in any emergency.'

Speer described to Kaufmann the chaotic situation in Berlin, telling him that he felt sure that the end was only a matter of days away. He also told him about his planned 'rebel's speech'. Kaufmann seized on the idea eagerly. 'You ought to deliver it. Why haven't you done so before?'

Speer explained the difficulties he had encountered and his fears of delivering the speech even now, with the Reich almost in ruins. But the energetic Kaufmann was not to be put off. 'Won't you give it on our Hamburg station? I can vouch for the technical head of our radio station. At least you can have the speech recorded at the station.' Speer swallowed hard. He had put his head on the chopping block once already and had, to his surprise, survived. Should he take another chance?

After a pause he nodded his head, 'I'll do it,' he said.

That same night Kaufmann took the Minister to the bunker in which the radio staff had set up their headquarters. It was late and most of the staff were already asleep. The two conspirators passed through one deserted room after another until they came to a small recording studio, occupied by two sound engineers.

Swiftly Kaufmann made the introductions. The two men shook Speer's hand perfunctorily but didn't bow as they would normally have done on being introduced to a minister of state. Speer realized that Kaufmann had briefed them on his treacherous act and the thought occurred to him that within a few minutes he would be completely at the mercy of these total strangers.

He looked at the text in his hands and then at the two men.

178

Their faces revealed nothing. Could he trust them? Would they talk if the Gestapo got them? He knew enough about the latter's methods to realize they didn't treat their prisoners with kid gloves. After a moment's consideration, he turned to Kaufmann and said he would go ahead with the speech, but he wanted the engineers to decide whether the record should be kept or destroyed once he had made his speech. The two men nodded in agreement, but their impassive faces revealed nothing of their emotions.

Opening with a description of the state of the German Nation that terrible spring, Albert Speer said, 'Never before in history has a civilized people been struck so hard, never have the destruction and war damage been so great as in our country, and never have a people borne the hardships of war with greater endurance, hardiness and loyalty than you. Now all of you are depressed, shaken to the core. Your love is turning to hate, your endurance and hardiness to fatigue and indifference.'

He paused and wiped his brow. The little cellar studio was hot and sticky with the heat generated by the electrical equipment. Speer swallowed hard and continued, 'This must not be. In this war the German people has displayed a determination which in days to come will, if history is just, be accorded the highest honour. Especially at this moment we must not weep and mourn for what is past. Only desperately hard work will enable us to bear our fate. But we can help ourselves by deciding realistically and soberly what the essential demands of the hour are.

'And here we find that there is only one main task—to avoid everything that could rob the German people of its basis for life, a basis already so diminished . . . In this phase of the war, therefore, we must avoid anything which could inflict further damage on our economy.'

Speer then went on to give out his orders for the preservation of what was left to Germany—its railways, roads, bridges, transport, etc., stating that 'to avoid injustices and serious blunders during this last phase of the war' certain important rules had to be observed. The last of these was, 'The activities of the Werewolf and similar organizations must cease at once. They give the enemy a just pretext for reprisals and also threaten the foundations of our strength as a nation. The survival of the German people is dependent on us meeting our obligations and maintaining order.' As he finished, Speer dropped his paper from his nerveless fingers and turned to the two engineers. For a moment no one spoke. The whirr of the machine filled the room until one of the engineers leaned over and clicked off the switch. It broke the spell.

'Well?' Speer asked.

One of the men shrugged, but neither spoke. Speer could see they were terrified by what they had just heard. Yet they did not object when he took the record and handed it to the waiting Kaufmann, who was as pale as the two engineers. Speer told him that he was to broadcast the record if anything happened to him, either on the orders of Bormann who hated him or at Hitler's own command. Licking his lips, he said, 'You will relay it at once if the Fuehrer is killed—or', he hesitated, 'the Werewolf kills me'.

And in those last days of April it appeared that Speer had good reason to fear that his life was in danger, for at last the Werewolves were let loose. Back in Heidelberg, his native city, Mayor Dr Neinhaus had been threatened with assassination by the Nazi resistance movement because he had surrendered the city to the Americans without a fight, after Speer had interceded with SS General Hausser to have the ancient university town declared an 'open city'.

Nor was Neinhaus the only man who had reason to fear the Werewolves. Other mayors had already been threatened with death or torture. In the newly-captured town of Giessen, two Werewolves, led by a Belgian SS officer, penetrated through the American lines and shot down a doctor who had 'collaborated' with the *Amis*. The new burgomaster of Elsdorf, who had already been granted permission to carry a personal weapon by the American occupiers, discovered the presence in his town of an ex-Gestapo official. Under cross-examination the latter confessed that he was aware of a Nazi order that all Rhenish burgomasters working for the Allies should be executed.

In the fighting around the Ruhr Pocket a top-secret German booklet was discovered which shocked those Allied Intelligence officers concerned with the Werewolf Organization. Entitled *Werwolf: Winke für Jagdeinheiten* (*Werewolf: Tips for Hunting Units*), it was the first official document from the secret organization to fall into Allied hands. The booklet gave a comprehensive account of how the Werewolves were to act behind the Allied lines in the execution of their major tasks, giving instructions about the 'liquidation' of German collaborators and (more importantly for the Allies) the sabotaging of Allied communications. Under the heading *Organization* the booklet stated:

'The special task of the hunting units is far-reaching and carefully planned missions to the enemy's rear. These hunting missions are the backbone of any small-scale war. Hunting units should be used to further local resistance movements.'

The worried Intelligence men wondered anxiously if this meant that the Werewolf organization had already established local partisan cells behind the Allied lines. The growing number of incidents far behind the Anglo-American front seemed to indicate that this was the case. More and more units, in particular those of the various rear echelons, began to report wires cut, roads sabotaged, trucks fired upon, supply dumps set on fire and the disappearance of individual soldiers who had been foolish enough to wander off by themselves. From the Third Army came the startling story that an American field hospital twenty miles behind the front had been captured by partisans and held for 72 hours. During this period (according to the report) all male members of the hospital had been murdered and the

Facsimile reproduction of one of the few documents ever captured by the Allies on the Werewolves. It is a training manual. *Werewolf: Hints for Hunting Units.* The illustration shows how the Werewolf should build a foxhole hideout.

female nurses raped, whereafter a nearby ammunition dump had been exploded, destroying the hospital.[1]

[1] In fact the hospital had been captured by regular SS troops who had killed an officer and two soldiers in the initial fight. Thereafter they had fled with the hospital's transport to a nearby ammo dump, which (although the dump's guards had fled in panic) they left unmolested in their haste to get away. As General Patton snorted when he heard of the 'atrocity', it 'is simply another illustration of my opinion that the report of no incident which happens after dark should be treated too seriously. They are always overstated.'

But although this story proved to be untrue there was no denying the participation of the civilian population in the defence of the city of Aschaffenburg. The fact that 'women and children lined the roof tops to pelt troops with hand grenades' (as General Bradley put it) seemed to confirm the intention of the 'hunting units' of the Werewolf Organization to enlist the aid of local resistance movements.

It was this sort of guerrilla action that accounted for the death of Montgomery's favourite liaison officer, 25-year-old John Poston of the 11th Hussars, who had been one of 'Monty's ears and eyes'[1] since North Africa. The young officer had never been one to fear danger; in fact, there were some at Montgomery's Tactical Headquarters who called him foolhardy. He was always discovering shortcuts along back roads which had not been reconnoitred. One day, however, he ran into a small group of fanatical German boys, who ambushed him from a ditch in the best Werewolf manner. Recklessly he drove his jeep straight at them, but, struck by a bullet, he skidded into a ditch where, bleeding to death, he fought until his last bullet was spent.

Back in Paris, SHAEF Intelligence hastily issued an instruction to all forward troops to be exceedingly careful in their dealings with the German civilian population, including the women and children, for (as the instructions stated) 'Your attitude towards women is wrong in Germany. Do you know German women have been trained to seduce you? Is it worth a knife in the back? A weapon can be concealed by women on the chest, between the breasts, or the abdomen, or the upper leg, under the buttocks, in a muff, in a handbag, in a hood or coat . . . How can you search women? The answer to that one is difficult. It may be your life at stake. You may find a weapon

---

[1] These were young battle-experienced British and American officers who carried out personal 'recces' at the front and reported directly to Montgomery. Montgomery was so moved by the young man's death that he wrote a personal letter to *The Times* stating 'There can be few young officers who have seen this war from the inside as did John Poston' and ending 'I was completely devoted to him and was very sad.'

by forcing them to pull their dress tight against their bodies here and there. If it is a small object you are hunting for, you must have another woman to do the searching and do it thoroughly in a private room.'

As one brigadier reported later, 'The reading aloud of this illuminating document enlivened many a bivouac.'

But if this pamphlet, which was widely circulated, caused merriment among the fighting troops who did not take the fears of the rear echelon regarding the Werewolves too seriously, putting it down to another example of the 'boys-behind-the-line's' remoteness from the 'real war', people like General Bradley were gravely worried.

On 24 April while the Russians encircled Berlin, Bradley was still convinced of the likelihood of the Werewolves' resistance in their Alpine Redoubt. That day he received a visit from a group of US congressmen who had been invited by Eisenhower to come to Europe and inspect for themselves the newly discovered German concentration camps. One of the visitors asked Bradley what the situation at the front was. Gloomily the General replied: 'We may be fighting one month from now and it may even be a year'.

Meanwhile, in Bavaria, General Patton was driving his men forward with reckless abandon, even making provision that the unblooded divisions should get into the fighting before 'it was all over'. On 22 April his III Corps headed for the Danube, and from thence planned to move on Linz and Salzburg in Austria. Although his intelligence officers were continually warning him to expect some terrible last-ditch weapon such as poison gas or a mysterious bomb which 'dissolved everything into dust', 'Blood and Guts' urged his men on with his usual energy. He believed neither in the Werewolf Movement nor in the Alpine Redoubt. For him the attack into Bavaria and Austria was 'simply a road march'. Now all that he was interested in was to get through the mythical Redoubt and on to Czechoslovakia, for as he was soon to confide to a bewildered Bradley, who asked him, 'Why does everyone in the Third Army want to liberate the Czechs?' 'Can't you see! The Czechs are our Allies and consequently their women aren't off limits. On to Czechoslovakia and fraternization!',[1] he yelled into the telephone, 'How in hell can you stop an army with a battle cry like that!'

General Patton had seen quite rightly that the war was over; the Germans were beaten.

VIII

Just after midnight on 24 April five black Horch automobiles drove up to a small house near a park in Lübeck, the medieval Hansa trading town on the Baltic coast. From the leading car stepped Heinrich Himmler followed by his bodyguard and the man whose organization had caused so many headaches for Allied Intelligence officers, SS General Pruetzmann.

Casting nervous glances to left and right to ensure that they had not been seen, the SS men hurriedly entered the little house. It was the Swedish consulate.

At the entrance they were met by Count Folke Bernadotte, who ushered Himmler and his aide, General Schellenberg, the man who had arranged the meeting, into a small candle-lit room. Hardly had they seated themselves when the high-pitched whistle of the air-raid warning filled the house. 'Shall we adjourn to the shelter?' the Swedish diplomat asked, watching Himmler's pale face by the light of the flickering candle.

Himmler hesitated for a moment and then decided to go and for an hour he went from person to person in the underground shelter asking them questions about what to do next, as if he were conducting a poll. Once Pruetzmann simply shrugged disdainfully and turned away from his boss, as if he could no

---

[1] As soon as Allied troops had reached Germany, Eisenhower had ordered no fraternization with the German civilians. Patton had not taken the measure seriously but Eisenhower had insisted he should ensure his men had no dealings with German women.

longer be bothered with Himmler's stupid importuning. Sharp-eyed Bernadotte, a member of the Swedish royal family, saw that the chief of the SS was exhausted and was having to use all his will power to keep calm.

Finally the British bombers flew away and the three men returned to the upper room. Courteously, Bernadotte offered his guests a drink, but Himmler would only take a soda; he had a passionate hatred of tobacco and alcohol. 'I realize that you're right,' he said suddenly. 'The war must end. I admit that Germany is defeated.'

Bernadotte remained silent, waiting for Himmler to say what he was thinking. Everything now depended upon the way the Allies treated the Germans, Himmler continued. 'In the present situation my hands are free. To save as much of Germany as possible from a Russian invasion, I'm willing to capitulate on the western front, but not on the eastern front. I have always been, and I shall always remain, a sworn enemy of Bolshevism.' He paused, and then asked Bernadotte if he would transmit his proposals to the Western Allies.

Bernadotte pursed his lips. He didn't feel that the West would buy the idea; they would want the fighting to finish on all fronts.

'I am well aware of how extremely difficult this is,' the SS leader replied, 'but all the same I want to make an attempt to save millions of Germans from a Russian occupation.'

In the end Bernadotte agreed to do as Himmler wished, but he asked what the German would do if the Allies did not accept the proposal.

Himmler did not hesitate. He said the words, as if he really believed them. 'In that event I shall take over command of the eastern front and be killed in battle.'

At the door of the consulate Himmler turned to the Count and displaying that petty bourgeois trait for always wanting to do the 'right thing', asked, 'Between men of the world, should I offer my hand to Eisenhower?'[1]

---

[1] He had previously said that he would like to meet Eisenhower and surrender to him personally.

The Count merely shrugged and Himmler turned and strode off to his car, followed by his bemedalled, polished entourage. This time he got behind the wheel of his Horch himself. Stepping down hard on the accelerator, as if he were eager to get away from the scene of his treachery, the car suddenly shot forward through a hedge and into the barbed-wire fence which surrounded the consulate. Himmler cursed and the cavalcade came to an abrupt halt while Swedish officials and SS officers pushed the car clear. At last Himmler lurched off shakily.

Closing the door behind the Germans, the Swedish aristocrat observed to his consular officials that there was something very symbolic about it all.

Although Himmler had remarked to Schellenberg and Pruetzmann that the meeting with Bernadotte to discuss the German surrender had been the 'bitterest day of my whole life,' his example caught on. While in Central Germany and in the surrounded capital, fanatical young men and women fought desperately under the Werewolf flag to stave off the inevitable defeat, risking being shot as spies or saboteurs, not only did their over-all Commander, Himmler, begin discussions with the enemy but Hans Pruetzmann himself set about independent negotiations with the West in a final attempt to save his neck.

A few days before Himmler had approached Bernadotte, Gauleiter Kaufmann had called together the Gauleiters of Schleswig-Holstein (Lohse), East Hanover (Telschow) and Weser-Emms (Wagener) and told them the unvarnished truth as he saw it, 'The state of the nation is hopeless. I don't believe the stuff that comes from Berlin. I suggest we surrender the whole north-east coast as quickly as possible to the western Allies so that they have the chance to overrun the Elbe area as far as Mecklenburg at once. Surely it's in all our interest that they occupy as much German territory on the right bank of the Elbe as possible before the Russians march in.' Then, turning to the senior Gauleiter present, he said, 'What do you think about it, Comrade Wegener?'

Wegener had always hated Kaufmann. More than once he had tried to denounce him to Berlin in the last few years. Now he had a golden opportunity to denounce his old enemy to Hitler as a traitor. But to Kaufmann's surprise, Wegener contented himself with shaking his head. The gesture could have been taken either for approval or disapproval. The other two Gauleiters took their cue from the senior man. They too made vague gestures which could have been interpreted several ways.

With that the meeting ended, leaving Kaufmann afraid that the other three might betray him at any time, and well aware that they would not support him in his attempt to surrender the whole of the River Elbe. In the end Kaufmann appealed to Pruetzmann, with the result that at the end of April involved discussions took place between Pruetzmann and Kaufmann at the same time as the latter was negotiating with Speer.

Thus Speer, who was afraid of being murdered by the Werewolves, yet determined to put a stop to their activities, was unknowingly associating with the Chief Werewolf, who himself now only wanted an end to the war and was prepared to approach the Danish underground in the pious hope they would make contact with the British to negotiate North Germany's surrender. And between both men was Gauleiter Kaufmann, who alone was aware of the two separate activities of the two men.

On 1 May, Admiral Doenitz, Hitler's one-time chief of U-boat warfare, took over the duties of chief-of-state after Hitler's suicide, setting up his headquarters in the old naval barracks in Flensburg, on the Danish–German border. Now with the Allies united on the Elbe, Germany was divided into two and only two pockets of major resistance remained to oppose the victorious Anglo–American armies in the south between Jugo–Slovakia and Austria; and in the north from the right bank of the River Elbe up to the Danish border.[1] Everywhere else the fighting was coming to an end. Field Marshal Schörner, who had been designated to command the non-

[1] Denmark and Norway were still in German hands.

existent Alpine Redoubt by one of Hitler's last orders, fled from the remains of his army, dressed in a sergeant's uniform, and did not go to the Redoubt. Otto Skorzeny made his way southwards to the Redoubt and found it did not exist, and that in his native Vienna a local revolution had broken out, just as it had in nearby Munich with Bavarians and Austrians firing on other Bavarians and Austrians. Skorzeny and a few companions fled into the mountains in disgust and waited till the *Amis* came to winkle him out.

But some of the most prominent Nazis did reach the Alpine Redoubt. In a final interview with fellow Austrian Adolf Eichmann, who had once boasted, 'I will gladly jump into my grave in the knowledge that five million enemies of the Reich (i.e. Jews) have already died like animals', scarfaced Gestapo-chief Ernst Kaltenbrunner asked him, 'What are you going to do now?'

Eichmann sipped his cognac thoughtfully, then said he thought he was going to go into the mountains and join the guerrillas.

'That's good. Good for the Reichsführer (he meant Himmler) too,' the towering Kaltenbrunner said with a sarcasm that went over Eichmann's head. 'Now he can take a different line in his negotiations with Eisenhower once he'll know that an Eichmann in the mountain will never surrender—*because he can't!*'

The ex-Gestapo chief, whose nerves had gone, banged down his cognac glass. 'It's all a lot of crap . . . The game's up.'

But if the heads of the Werewolf and their fellow high-ranking Nazi officials realized that the war was over, the fanatical young men and women who had believed so implicitly in the Nazi creed did not. In the territory still left to the Germans, they fought a bitter small-scale war of their own while, all around, regular German formations were surrendering by the thousand and the hundred thousand. At Daerstorf, the 'Desert Rats'[1] intent on accepting the surrender of Hamburg

---

[1] The British 7th Armoured Division, which gained its nickname from its divisional patch.

which Kaufmann had finally achieved, bumped into one such group, but as the official divisional history put it succinctly, 'the experiment was not repeated'.

Further north, a group of SS men supported by youthful Werewolves refused to give themselves up to the Seventh's running mate, the 11th Armoured Division. Digging themselves in the Forst Segeberg, a well-wooded area, they prepared to make a fight of it against two battalions of British troops. Even when, a few days later, Admiral Doenitz in Flensburg ordered them to surrender, they refused to until finally in desperation the German Command ordered its own 8th Parachute Division into action against them. Then at last they gave in, but not before the woods were filled with their dead bodies, a cruel commentary on their lost hopes and their betrayal by their leaders.

On the other side of the Elbe the last fugitives from the Werewolf school at Gatow fought their way to the river in ten-man teams, made up of soldiers and civilians, male and female. But the sight of British and American soldiers on the other side of the water barrier waiting for them, made them turn back. With the pathetic handful of weapons at their disposal they tried to hold off the leading elements of the victorious Russian horde. But their resistance did not last long. The Russian tanks swept through them as if they did not exist, though a few of those who managed to dig themselves in, in the already prepared underground bunkers, survived a little longer till their own fellow citizens betrayed the sites of their food dumps to the Russians and were allowed to plunder them as a reward.[1]

---

[1] My informant on this stage of the Werewolf resistance left her bag, containing her bank-book, behind in her underground bunker as she fled. Ten years later safely established in West Germany, her Werewolf past long forgotten, she received a polite note from East Germany (the signature was indecipherable) requesting her to come to a certain city there to 'collect her savings'. Needless to say she did not go. But, obviously, the Russian or East German authorities were still interested in the Nazi underground organization as late as 1955.

But even the most fanatical of the young people eventually became aware of reality. At the end of the first week of May, 1945, the guns began to grow silent everywhere, and the lone fighters lost heart. On 3 May Speer broadcast his 'rebel's speech', but Doenitz did not allow him to use the Werewolf broadcasting post: the Admiral felt it would not be politic since it might sabotage the morale of the German troops still fighting on the Eastern Front. Two days later, Doenitz himself broadcast from Radio Copenhagen, Flensburg and Prague and said, among other things, 'The fact that at present an armistice reigns means that I must ask every German man and woman to stop any illegal activity in the Werewolf or other such organizations in those territories occupied by the Western Allies because this can only injure our people.'[1]

On the same day Field Marshal Keitel, who had fled Hitler's HQ in Berlin, ordered the German Luftwaffe not to engage in any Werewolf action, an action strongly supported by the new Fuehrer, Doenitz, who, just in time, stopped a Luftwaffe squadron from 'going underground',[2] though they were not able to prevent individual pilots fleeing with their planes to neutral countries, in particular Franco's Spain.

Silently and sadly the betrayed survivors of those 4,000 to 5,000 young men and women, who had volunteered for the Werewolves two months before, hid or threw away their weapons and began to make their way home to a world which, in their opinion, had been irrevocably destroyed.

Hennemann and Wenzel had not reached *Gut Hombusch* without experiencing their share of misadventures. For twenty-four hours they had waited in vain for Heidorn and the others and when at last they set out they had repeatedly lost their way. But now the three survivors were reunited, and after resting up

[1] It is interesting to note that the order did *not* apply to Russian-occupied territories.

[2] I have not been able to find out whether this was the 252 Squadron which dropped the Operation Carnival team.

long enough for Heidorn to regain his strength, they set out once more for the Rhine.

When they reached the river, Wenzel, for reasons known only to himself refused to go any further. Instead he remained behind at a lonely farm near the village of Stommeln, about a mile away from the river. The farm, *Gut Velderhof*, was one of the hiding places that had been recommended to the members of 'Operation Carnival' before they had left Hülchrath and Wenzel felt safe there.

Nevertheless, during his stay at the farm, he never once left it, even to go to the nearest village. He worked hard in the fields with the owner, Barthel Schumacher, occasionally playing a hand of cards with the others in the evening, but usually keeping very much to himself. Herr Schumacher, who later told the British investigators that 'he was a hard worker and skilled. He was invariably polite and helpful, and one could notice from his manners that he came from a good home', asked him one day while they were working side by side in a field if he had been an officer. Wenzel volunteered the information that he had held the rank of first lieutenant. That was all.

The only person who managed to get more out of him was Agnes Meisen, a maid on the farm. Wenzel was interested in the pretty girl and in a moment of unusual confidence told her that he came from South-West Africa where his parents had a farm and that he had an uncle in Halberstadt in the new Russian Occupation Zone. But when she pressed him further Wenzel shut up like a clam. Wenzel had plans, and was as reserved with his new associates as he had been throughout that long last winter of the war with his old ones of 'Operation Carnival'. *Wenzel intended to survive*.

Early in August, 1945, he finally left *Velderhof*. He left without ceremony, telling Schumacher that he intended to make his way to his uncle in Halberstadt who, as the police later discovered, did not exist. The cunning ex-leader of the Aachen murder team crossed the Rhine and disappeared for good. No trace of him was ever found again.

192

Hennemann and Heidorn succeeded in swimming the Rhine only to be picked up by an American patrol and sent, of all places, to an internment camp at Aachen. There, however, they succeeded in convincing their captors that they were harmless and were soon once again fleeing from the scene of their crime in an effort to return to their wives in what was soon to become the Russian Zone of Occupation.

Morgenschweiss recovered from his wounds with remarkable speed. In spite of his apparently delicate constitution he had considerable reserves of strength and after only ten days in hospital he found refuge with an old Hitler Youth friend in the village of Mechernich. Here he openly boasted of his exploits during 'Operation Carnival', but no one believed him. As Theo Sechtem, his friend, later told the police, 'he was always telling stories and we thought it was another of them'. Disgruntled, Erich decided it was time to go home to his parents.

Ilse Hirsch took longer to recover. Her lungs were failing badly and she had to enter a sanitorium for a long period. Finally she was released from hospital and after staying with a woman who had befriended her in the ward, she took the opportunity presented by a truck driving to Hamm, her home town, to return to her parents.[1]

For Pruetzmann there was no longer any hope of survival. After a disastrous meeting with the new German Fuehrer, when Himmler had pleaded to be allowed to become 'the second man in your state', and Doenitz[2] had refused, Pruetzmann realized that there was no further place for him in Flensburg.[3]

---

[1] From whence she would soon return to Euskirchen, some dozen miles from Aachen, to take up her old pre-war job in the Umbreit bookshop as if 'Operation Carnival' and all that went with it had never even happened.

[2] The Admiral, alarmed at Himmler's appearance at his HQ in the company of his SS bodyguard and leading members of his entourage, had hidden a pistol under the papers on his desk and was prepared to shoot it out with Himmler if the worst came to the worst. It didn't. Himmler left timidly after Doenitz declined his services.

[3] He had found himself a completely useless post as 'liaison' officer between Doenitz and Himmler although the former was completely disinterested and had not the least desire to 'liaise' with Himmler.

On 5 May, Himmler held his last staff conference at Flensburg. All the high ranking SS, SD and Gestapo generals, police leaders, *Obergruppenführer* and *Gruppenführer* attended like—as Trevor Roper put it—'obsolete dinosaurs, moving inappropriately in the wrong geological age'. Himmler told the assembled officers with their portentous titles from organizations which were already defunct, that he still saw 'political possibilities' for the organization. He intended to establish a 'reformed' Nazi administration, which would negotiate with the Allies. In the meantime, the SS would have to be dissolved, although its leaders could join him as 'advisers' if they wished.

Pruetzmann shared the opinion of another SS general there, who remarked afterwards 'the possibilities of which he spoke make me clutch my head'. He had to get away, but how and to what country? For a few days the chief of the Werewolves toyed with the idea of trying to escape by submarine. Some of the U-boats were still available and manned by disgruntled crews who would chance anything to escape from the wreck of the Third Reich. But when Doenitz refused to allow a U-boat crew to run the Allied blockade to Spain with Gauleiter Lohse of Cologne, who a few months before had seconded Ilse Hirsch to the Werewolf Organization, he knew that possibility was ruled out. He next considered escape by air, but the only machines, Condors, which could make a long flight were stationed in Norway.[1]

In the end Pruetzmann resigned himself to the inevitable. A few days later he allowed himself to be captured by the British, but the thought of having to spend the rest of his life in internment camps, such as the one in which he now found himself, was apparently too much for him. Though he was thoroughly searched before he entered the camp, he managed to smuggle in a cyanide capsule. Twenty-four hours after he

---

[1] The only one known to have made the attempt escaped with the Belgian SS General Leon Degrelle and it crash-landed just off the Spanish coast after running out of fuel. Degrelle survived and to-day lives in Madrid.

194

had surrendered, he swallowed it in the latrine. He died within minutes, taking the secrets of the Werewolves with him.

Now at last it was the turn of Heinrich Himmler himself. The man who had conceived of the Werewolves and a half a dozen similar organizations which had struck terror into so many hearts throughout Europe in these last terrible years had come a long way since the time when as a nineteen-year-old youth in Munich he had been accused of murdering his prostitute mistress. The case against him was dismissed for lack of evidence. He married a woman who was seven years his senior. But both the marriage and the chicken farm he started with his wife's money failed and the frustrated chicken farmer turned to politics and became a Nazi. His rise thereafter was meteoric and before long he was the most feared man in the Nazi administration.

Now it was time that he paid the bill. But Himmler, who had sent so many German youngsters to their death for the 'greater glory of the Fatherland,' still hoped to avoid capture. Rather than give himself up, he decided to flee from Flensburg.

'But you can't just walk out,' SS General Ohlendorf protested when his chief announced his intention. 'You must make a radio speech or send some declaration to the Allies that you take responsibility for what's happened. You must give the reasons.'

Himmler agreed to do this, but it was only to calm the irate ex-Gestapo chief. A little while later he encountered one of Doenitz's 'new cabinet', ex-Rhodes Scholar Schwerin von Krosigk and asked anxiously, 'Please tell me what is going to become of me?'

The man looked at him with contempt, 'I'm not interested in the least what will happen to you or any other man. Only our mission interests me, not our personal destinies.' The Count who was keeping control of himself only by strict will-power and the repeated injunction 'discipline, gentlemen, discipline', continued, 'It must not happen that the Reichsführer decks himself out with a false name and a false beard. If I were you I'd drive up to Montgomery and say, 'Here I am,

Himmler the SS general, ready to take responsibility for all my men.'

Himmler was reduced to silence by this but that same night he told his circle of intimates cryptically that he still had one great mission left. 'For years I have borne a great burden. This new great task I shall have to undertake alone. One or two of you perhaps can accompany me.'

Heinrich Himmler, the last of Hitler's Werewolves, had chosen the 'false name and false beard' as the easier way out and, shaving off his moustache and wearing a patch over one eye, he assumed the name of Heinrich Hitzinger, whose pass he had obtained after he had been executed.

With a few faithful followers, Himmler made his way through Holstein, moving southwards. The group successfully crossed the Elbe, but were stopped at a British checkpoint by the Redcaps who had been warned to keep a lookout for Himmler. Thus it was that at 2 pm on 23 May Himmler and his group were delived to Interrogation Camp No 031 near Luneburg.

The new arrivals were paraded in front of Captain Tom Selvester, formerly of the Reconnaissance Corps. Three of them immediately caught his eye, two were tall and smart, but the third was, as he remarked later, 'a small, miserable-looking and shabbily dressed man'.

He ordered the three to step forward. The shabby little man looked somehow familiar. Ordering the guards to remove the two big men, he began to question the third. Then, in Selvester's own words, 'the small man who was wearing a black patch over his left eye removed the patch and put on a pair of spectacles. His identity was at once obvious and he said "Heinrich Himmler" in a very quiet voice.'

Swiftly Captain Selvester alerted 21st Army Group Intelligence and two officers were rushed down from Luneburg. They were followed that evening by Colonel Michael Murphy, chief of Secret Intelligence at Montgomery's HQ. The experienced Intelligence man immediately concluded that the former head of the SS had a poison capsule hidden about his person. In fact, Selvester's camp doctor had already found one phial of poison hidden in Himmler's shabby clothing.

Murphy, however, was not satisfied. He ordered the doctor to examine Himmler once more. The MO, on Murphy's advice, ordered the German to open his mouth. Obediently Himmler did as he was told and, at the back of his mouth, the doctor saw a small black object.

'Turn your head to the light,' he ordered and when Himmler, who did not speak English, did not react, he began to twist his head towards the naked bulb burning overhead.

Himmler pulled his head way. His eyes were full of tears and he snapped his teeth together with a crunch. Inside his mouth the hidden phial of cyanide burst, releasing its deadly contents and, before the horrified eyes of the British MO, *Reichsführer* Heinrich Himmler sank slowly to the stone floor, his pale face now flushed an ugly crimson, his thin fingers clutching at his throat as he fought desperately for breath. Seconds later he was dead, as the shocked group of British officers stared down at his body. The men who had conceived the idea of Hitler's Werewolves had committed suicide and the fantastic, impossible adventure, fated to failure from the very start, was over.

Epilogue

'A rabble of boy scouts.'

German General Westphal on the
Werewolves. May, 1945

The Aachen 'Werewolf Trial' started inauspiciously enough. The American CIC had made little attempt to find the murderers of Franz Oppenhoff. They had contented themselves with examining the murdered mayor's intimates and family, and passing on their suspicions to the British[1] that Dr Faust was probably connected with the crime somehow or other. That was that. It was, after all, easy enough to find a replacement for the murdered Mayor.

The British were not so sanguine. They had begun looking into the case as soon as the war ended. What started them on their search for the murderers is no longer known. Morgenschweiss's fellow Werewolves were of the opinion that the loudmouthed youth had blabbed when he had been arrested by the British as a suspected Nazi late in 1945. Erich Morgenschweiss, for his part, maintained that as Hennemann, Hirsch and Gutenberger were already in British custody in 1945 why should he be regarded as the one who had betrayed them to the occupiers?

Be that as it may, on 14 February, 1947, Dr Heitzer, Aachen's Public Prosecutor, received a brief note from the British Resident Officer, Major Gale, stating that he should 'attend Major Gale at nine o'clock precisely on the following Thursday or Friday'.

No further details were given or apparently expected by Dr Heitzer. He made his appearance and was told by the British Security Officer that a boy named Erich Morgenschweiss, who was in British custody, was suspected of having murdered the first Allied Burgomaster of Aachen, Herr Oppenhoff. Major Gale told Heitzer that the British authorities were not prepared to make out a case against Morgenschweiss. The shooting of young Josef Saive was 'an act of war'; as for Oppenhoff, Gale said, he had been told to pass on the information in British possession to the Germans. What should happen from then on was up to the Germans themselves.

[1] Aachen became part of the British Zone of Occupation in May, 1945.

Dr Heitzer was obviously excited by the possibilities of the case. In his memorandum dictated on the same day as he had the interview with Major Gale, he stated:

'After receipt of all the documents relevant to the case, I intend to examine the accused and all the witnesses myself in order to obtain a picture of their personalities and their reliability.

In the light of the great importance of this case not only for the Military Government but also for the German People, I intend to conduct the whole business myself and appear in court as prosecutor.'

Whatever one might think of Dr Heitzer's reasons for pursuing the case of which the British had already washed their hands, it must be stated that he set to work with remarkable thoroughness. The five bulky files pertaining to the case showed that he left no stone unturned in his attempts to find the murderers and their motives.

One by one, he found the Werewolves and the men who had trained them. Gutenberger was easy; he was already in British hands serving a 12-year sentence for war crimes. Hennemann was soon captured and was interned in the same camp as Morgenschweiss. Ilse Hirsch was also found and imprisoned without difficulty. In fact, with a trace of that blind fanaticism that had made her volunteer for the murder mission, she told the officers who came to arrest her that 'an old lady came into the Umbreit shop and told me that the Aachen Public Prosecutor was looking for me. If I'd wished I could have escaped.' Instead she stayed to face the music. Of all the accused she was the only one who gave an honest account of her role during Operation Carnival.

Lt-Col Neinhaus was also questioned, as were Skorzeny and Stubenrauch, the Gestapo man who had prepared the faked papers for the team. Then Raddatz was discovered, working as an interpreter for the British troops in Siegen. Not far away in Bückeburg, Heidorn, who had returned from the Russian

Zone after divorcing his wife, was found working in, of all places, the kitchen of the local RAF Malcolm Club!

But it proved impossible to trace SS Lieutenant Herbert Wenzel, although the persistent Dr Heitzer checked with every German and Austrian university. He discovered the whereabouts of Hella, his mistress of the Düsseldorf days, as well as the blonde teenage hair-dresser in Hildesheim. He also requested that the Soviet Zone Police check suspects in the whole Halberstadt area. All was to no avail. Early in 1948 he did receive a letter from a former French Foreign Legionnaire in Bremen maintaining that he had met an ex-SS lieutenant named Wenzel in North Africa, who was now 'Sergeant-Chef at the Training Depot at Sidi-bel-Abbes'. But nothing came of the lead and in the end Dr Heitzer had to be satisfied with arraigning Gutenberger, Raddatz, Stubenrauch, Hennemann, Heidorn and Hirsch. Morgenschweiss would appear for the prosecution as a witness.

The trial opened to a packed court on Thursday 18 October, 1949, in a Germany which had just regained its independence as 'The Federal Republic'. In spite of the fact that the newly independent Germans were sick of 'war trials', the Oppenhoff Case, in which Germans had murdered another German, caused a great deal of interest and virtually every major newspaper and magazine was represented in the court.

But if the eager spectators expected any sensational disclosures on the first day they were disappointed. Dr Lambertz, the Public Prosecutor who had replaced Dr Heitzer, contented himself with a routine examination of the accused, merely obtaining the statement from Gutenberger that he held the operation 'to have been legally justified' and that Himmler had twice ordered him to get on with the job. Hennemann told the court that his job had been solely to guide the group. Heidorn supported him in this statement, maintaining that they had not known Wenzel's real intentions until it had been too late. At this Dr Lambertz allowed himself a mild smile of disbelief, a feeling that was shared by most of the spectators.

The following day Heidorn's divorced wife appeared as a witness for the prosecution and stated that when her husband had come home on leave from Hildesheim he had shown her a fake pass, a large amount of foreign currency and told her that within twenty-four hours he would parachute out over Aachen to carry out a 'great deed'. When she asked him if he meant he was going to drop bombs on the town or execute someone, Heidorn had answered 'she would soon find out'. Stubenrauch also undermined the defence when he stated that he had a conversation with Wenzel in which the latter had complained, 'I've been given a very unpleasant job. I'd rather try to blow up an enemy command post with a row of hand grenades tied to my waist, than risk the lives of five people for the sake of that rogue' [i.e. Oppenhoff].

Lambertz then called Morgenschweiss. He told the boy publicly, 'You are not accused yet and are going to be questioned as a witness'[1] which said categorically that all the accused knew what was going on. He then went on to give details about how each of the accused had spoken of the intended murder prior to their departure from Hildesheim. Gutenberger, Raddatz, Stubenrauch, Heidorn, Hennemann, Hirsch—they'd all known they were to be dropped over Aachen.

As Dr Lambertz was to say a few days later in his final summing up:

'I maintain that all the accused knew what the purpose of the mission was. The whole team had weeks to consider what they were about. It hardly seems credible that they did not discuss their mission.'

But Dr Lambertz did not have it all his own way in that third week of the trial, for Hennemann's lawyer, Frau Doctor

[1] Morgenschweiss, unknown to his fellow Werewolves, was in a difficult position. Some time before, when backing a truck, he had run over and killed an elderly man. Through Dr Lambertz's influence he had got away with a fine of 108 marks. He therefore, felt indebted to the Public Prosecutor.

Oehlert, had made a speciality of defending accused National Socialists in her home town of Hamburg, and was the only one of the six defending lawyers who refused to accept the state's case. Calling both Op de Hit and Faust to the witness stand, she asked the two men, both of whom had once served under Oppenhoff in the first Allied-appointed administration of the city, 'Would it not be possible to describe Oppenhoff as a deserter? Wasn't he still a soldier when he took over his office. Did he not still have a Wehrmacht pass? Didn't he carry out a task which went beyond his normal duties as a citizen? Isn't it true that the essential factor was that Oppenhoff escaped from his military duties?'

She hammered the questions home in a manner which shocked the court, but the lawyer was not in the least worried by the reaction of Catholic Aachen which had since come to regard the dead Mayor as a democratic hero, one of the first, indeed, in post-war Germany.[1]

Op de Hit and Faust paled under her attack but maintained their position that Oppenhoff and they had only agreed to serve under the Allies in order to protect the best interests of those Aacheners left in the ruined city after its surrender.

A member of Oppenhoff's city council, Dr Breuer, stated that 'we felt that we had a duty to look after the population in the best manner possible. We never thought that we were supposed to spy for the Americans. Oppenhoff told [me] he had never possessed a uniform.'

It was at this juncture that Dr Oehlert created a sensation by producing as a witness Dr Lennertz, lawyer and a former colleague of Oppenhoff, who maintained that he had seen the latter in Army uniform two days before the evacuation of Aachen. That was on 12 September, 1944.

The announcement shook the prosecution and created an

[1] Dr Oehlert was to regret her aggressiveness, since it took many years before the City of Aachen paid her her legal fees and travel expenses. Indeed in the end she was forced to issue a summons against the official concerned for 'negligence of duty' before she received her money.

uproar among the spectators. If Oppenhoff had been a soldier then he was a traitor, or at least a deserter, who, under the regulations pertaining in Nazi Germany at that particular time, was liable to be executed without trial. It was exactly the excuse all the defendants had used to justify their actions.

Hurriedly Frau Oppenhoff was called to the witness box once more to testify vaguely, 'My husband had been released from the Army at that time. It could be that because of the enmity of the Nazi District Leader [Schmeer] that he was regarded as being on leave.'[1]

But a triumphant Oehlert could see that at least the Press did not believe her. Her defence had had it effect.

Dr Oehlert went on to state in defence of her clients that, 'he (Oppenhoff) was a tool of the enemy invaders and supported their military aims and plans in that he helped to build up a civil administration. This activity, in addition to his aid to the enemy in their efforts to root out German soldiers and officials still in Aachen, must be regarded as an attempt to destroy the fighting spirit (of the German forces). And all this took place at a time when many Aacheners were still dying in the ranks of the German Wehrmacht.

'The whole case . . . is really intended as a justification for Oppenhoff. This motive is so apparent that one has the feeling that it forms the basis of the whole affair.'

Nevertheless it was Dr Lambertz for the prosecution who won the case in the end. The Werewolf team was pronounced guilty by the judges.[2]

Thus it was that at twenty minutes to three on the afternoon of 24 October, the chairman of the court, Doctor Maas,

---

[1] Oppenhoff's former employer testified that after many attempts to keep the future chief burgomaster from being called up, he was ordered to report to the Luftwaffe air base at Wengerohr, near the town of Wittlich, but after an absence of some three days he returned and took up his former employment. This had been in August, 1944.

[2] German legal procedure is different from that of the Anglo-Saxon courts; there are usually three professional judges and six lay ones, who act as a kind of jury.

commenced the reading of the sentences to a packed court. For the last time the Werewolves (bar, of course, Wenzel) were all together. Raddatz was accompanied by his wife; Ilse Hirsch sat with her sister and her fiancé. Hennemann, Heidorn and Stubenrauch were alone. Gutenberger sat in the prisoner's box under guard. None of them looked across at Morgen-schweiss who stared at them defiantly.

Dr Maas began by saying that 'a thousand years ago a secret court could declare someone *vogelfrei*, these days are long passed'. He then went on to examine the motives of the Were-wolves, remarking that Ilse Hirsch had obviously believed in the Nazi principle that the 'State and individual are one . . . and everything is legal which is of aid to Germany and ordered from above.'

He looked at the woman as he said this, but Ilse Hirsch, her face as pale as ever, did not seem to notice his glance. In the case of Raddatz and Gutenberger, Dr Maas went on, things were different. They would have had Oppenhoff shot whether the order had come from Himmler or not. That was clear from their long-term planning of the assassination. As for Heidorn and Hennemann, they had known what they had been about and could have got out of their mission if they had wished once they reached Aachen.[1]

Making reference to Dr Oehlert's accusation that Oppenhoff had been a traitor, Dr Maas said, 'His work for his suffering fellow citizens cannot be allowed to be overshadowed by any suspicion that he was a traitor.' Then he passed the sentences: Karl Gutenberger received four years, Karl Raddatz three; Hennemann was sentenced to eighteen months and Heidorn got one year.

Ilse Hirsch and Johannes Stubenrauch were set free after

---

[1] In his defence Hennemann had told the court that Wenzel had said to him in Hülchrath, 'I want you to guide us through the enemy lines on a dangerous mission. Any attempt on your part to defect—and I shall be forced to use my authority.' Hennemann had interpreted this as meaning that Wenzel would have shot him without ceremony.

Dr Maas had pointed out that no one should draw the conclusion because of the mildness of the sentences that the court approved of the Nazis. The motivation of the court had been that 'a well-regulated code of justice could not allow the blind assassination of political opponents whatever the motives of the assassins were'. The trial was over.

In effect, none of the accused, save Karl Gutenberger, served their sentences. Under the determined leadership of Dr Oehlert, the accused men's lawyers fought the sentence and in 1952 managed to have it reduced to a few months in each case so that the accused, who immediately after the war had all done time in internment camps, were released forthwith.

To-day they are all alive and prosperous, save Karl Gutenberger, who died in 1961 (though he, too, managed to build up a thriving wholesale business before he passed away). Ilse Hirsch is married to a civil servant and has two teenage children. She lives only twenty miles or so away from the scene of the most momentous event in her life. Karl Raddatz ended up teaching, as Karl Gutenberger had predicted in 1945. To-day he is a retired *Oberstudienrat*—'a senior grammar school teacher'—who is proud of his final title and does not want to be reminded of that other one of which he was so proud long ago—*SS Standartenführer*. Heidorn is still working, but Hennemann has retired. Erich Morgenschweiss is as youthful as ever in spite of his forty-two years. In these last few years he has tried a lot of jobs without too much success. For a while he was on the road selling margarine in the very border area where he was once sweating for his young life. But he didn't like it much. 'Too much rushing around and excitement. Not good for you', he tells you confidentially in his tight little apartment in a working class street with his wife working on a loom in the far corner of the room 'making a little money on the side'. Now he has a steady job in a little town near Aachen.

Does he ever think of those exciting days when he was a member of the Werewolves? He shakes his blond head vigorously. 'No, that's all over. All I know is that I never go in the woods around here. They're still dangerous.' He means the mines and perhaps he is right. In the woods between Aachen and the little town in which he lives a good thousand explosive devices are found annually. 'Would he do it again?' you ask him after the *Pils und Schnaps*[1] have had their effect.

Erich Morgenschweiss runs his hands through his wavy hair. Over the years his shoulders have broadened unnaturally so that there is something gorrilla-like about him when he stands up. Then he shakes his head slowly. 'No, I wouldn't. I'd never join anything like the Werewolves again. In fact I wouldn't join anything except . . .'

'Except what?'

'The fishing club—where you can be by yourself and away from people. That's the only club *I'd* ever join . . .'

And perhaps Erich Morgenschweiss is right. He and the rest of Hitler's Werewolves were brutally tricked by those in authority in the last days of the dying Third Reich, who, while they still loudly mouthed the slogans of victory and resistance to the death, were already preparing for defeat. They knew that the Alpine Redoubt, which so frightened Eisenhower and his advisers, was non-existent, and, therefore, the Werewolves would not have an 'impregnable bastion' from which to sally to carry out their deadly work in the Allies' rear.

Thus it was that of all the conquered nations in Europe[2] during World War Two, Hitler's Germany—the one people committed officially to 'Total War'—tamely handed in its weapons in May, 1945, and set about the task of rebuilding its shattered country. Within two weeks of the German surrender, the Allied order requiring the troops to carry their personal weapons with them at all times, on and off duty, was rescinded. The average Tommy or GI was as safe in Hamburg or Frankfurt or in the villages and woods of the newly occupied country

[1] Beer and spirits.
[2] In 1940 even the United Kingdom had already set up the nucleus of a guerrilla organization which would go into operation if the Germans invaded and conquered the island country.

as he would have been in his hometown. Hitler's feared Werewolves had simply gone home and resumed their normal peacetime existences.

'As if,' as General Siegfried Westphal, the last German Chief-of-Staff in the West, said contemptuously when he was captured in May, 1945, 'what the Wehrmacht had failed to do could be accomplished by a rabble of Boy Scouts'.

It is a fitting enough epitaph on Hitler's Werewolves—'a rabble of boy scouts'.